Looking Back the Efforts on Decentralization in India

About the Author

Prof. Ganapathy Palanithurai, Rajiv Gandhi Chair for Panchayati Raj studies, Department of Political Science and Development Administration, Gandhigram Rural Institute—Deemed University, Gandhigram is an academic activist working with academic community, civil society, policy community and political community to impress upon them the importance and need of democratic local governance in India to enable the poor to lead a decent dignified human life. All his academic, research and outreach activities are being supported by an array of funding agencies namely the World Bank, the UNDP, the UNICEF, the Hunger Project, SDC, DANIDA, Action Aid International, the Ford Foundation, Population Foundation of India, the Rajiv Gandhi Foundation, Toolkit Foundation—Netherland, Ministry of Panchayati Raj and State Planning Commission. He was a visiting Professor in Cologne University, Germany. He has to his credit seventy three books, 126 research articles, 112 popular articles in popular newspapers, 83 monographs published in a span of three decades. He is the coordinator of UGC-SAP and UGC innovative programme. He held several administrative positions like Dean, Faculty of Social Sciences, Dean, Student's Welfare, Member, Syndicate, Member Senate, Member, and Academic Council in Gandhigram Rural Institute. He was and is member of many advisory committees of the Government of India and Government of Tamil Nadu pertinent to local government and rural development.

Looking Back the Efforts on Decentralization in India

G. Palanithurai

CONCEPT PUBLISHING COMPANY PVT. LTD.
NEW DELHI-110059

ISBN-13: 978-93-5125-299-3

First Published 2017

Published and Printed by

Concept
Since 1974

Concept Publishing Company Pvt. Ltd.
A/15-16, Commercial Block, Mohan Garden,
New Delhi-110059 (INDIA)
T: +91 11 25351460, +91 11 25351794
E: publishing@conceptpub.com, *W*: www.conceptpub.com

Cataloging in Publication Data—DK Courtesy: D.K. Agencies (P) Ltd. <docinfo@dkagencies.com>

Palanithurai, G., author.
Looking back the efforts on decentralization in India / G. Palanithurai.
pages cm
Includes bibliographical references and index.
ISBN 9789351252993

1. Decentralization in government—India. 2. Local government—India. 3. Panchayat—India. I. Title.

JS7009.P35 2017 DDC 320.840954 23

Preface

Decentralization in India became a bone of contention since the days of freedom struggle. It was considered as a government machinery, a governance mechanism, an administrative strategy, a management tool for effective delivery of services. Perceptions vary across people, countries and segments. When decentralization was conceptualized during the freedom struggle with the concept 'Panchayati Raj' or Gram Swaraj given by M.K. Gandhi and it was opposed by Dr. B.R. Ambedkar, the whole world conceptualized nation building through centralization. When the countries were in nation building process, they considered the decentralization was antithetical to nation building. Hence, serious attention was not given despite the efforts of the political pundits. Apart from the above India was struggling to build a nation after the partition of Pakistan and merger of principalities. The above two factors have seriously hampered the idea of strengthening the grassroots institutions as units of governance. Later, it was conceptualized as an administrative machinery to deliver services to the community as it was the need of the hour. After Independence steps had been taken to strengthen the Panchayati Raj system but, success was not to the level of the expectation of the political pundits. Decentralization at present is conceptualized and operationalized with different perspectives in the countries of the world. Now, it becomes a global phenomenon. Decentralization, globalization, democratization are becoming movements. They are independent to each other, but they are interlinked and interrelated. Form and content of decentralization depend on the need of the society and understanding of the policy community. This phenomenon is applicable to the Afro-Asian countries in the present context. It is proved beyond doubt that decentralization is the best instrument to achieve inclusive governance and inclusive development. Yet, it does not take place as expected.

But, now the whole world started moving from centralization to decentralization with an objective of achieving equitable development with the active participation of stakeholders and to deepen democracy. To realize the above objectives, countries have adopted different strategies and created different institutional structures and mechanisms.

Althrough decentralization efforts since Independence have not succeeded fully and hence this time India has followed a sustainable local governance institution by amending the Constitution of the country. By doing so, it becomes part of the Constitution as Central and State Governments. For the past twenty years, the Central Government have taken series of steps to strengthen the local governance system in India. Many of the State Governments also have taken efforts to strengthen local governance system. Where are the local governance institutions in India today? How are they functioning? Have they fulfilled the objectives with which they have been created? What are the bottlenecks in the decentralization process? What are the problems involved in strengthening the local governance system in India? Are the daunting questions linkering in the minds of the researchers. Having worked with local bodies for the past two decades, I tried to cover entire gamut of decentralization process from the perspective of local bodies. Along with the local bodies, I worked with the policy communities, media representatives, and civil society organizations and hence, based on my experience, I try to narrate the journey of decentralization. Last one year, I have been asked by different institutions to share my reflections based on my experiences. Lectures delivered and papers presented in different research institutions have been edited to make it a small monograph. Thus, it has come as a book. All the chapters packed in this volume have some repetitions which are unavoidable.

G. Palanithurai

Acknowledgements

If I am able to reflect on decentralization meaningfully, I must be thankful to many individuals and institutions who enabled me to make such ventures. I have been provided with volley of literatures by different institutions, organizations and individuals on decentralization. As I have been working with local body leaders and policy communities, I have been ably assisted by some institutions and individuals continuously by providing needed informations, documents and perspectives. Since, I have something to argue on this subject based on my work in the past. I have been invited by various institutions for interaction on this subject. These invitations made me to visit the fields and read the relevant literatures repeatedly. The World Bank, The Ford Foundation, UNDP, IDS, UK, European Union, Ministry of Panchayati Raj, Government of India, Institute of Social Sciences, New Delhi, PRIA, New Delhi, The Hunger Project, New Delhi and a few other institutions deserve my appreciation as they assisted me. Equally, S.M. Vijayanand now Chief Secretary and Former Secretary, Government of India, Dr. S.S. Meenakshisundaram, Former Secretary, Ministry of Rural Development, Government of India, Manishankar Aiyar, Member of Parliament, Ragunanthan, Former Joint Secretary, Government of India, Hari K. Nagarajan, IRMA Anand, Manoj Rai, PRIA, New Delhi, Dr. Jos Chathukulam, CRM, Kottayam and a few others deserve my gratitude as they constantly interacted with me.

I have to mention a few institutions which have invited me for interaction and presentation. They are: Kerala Institute of Local Administration, Kerala, and Centre for Studies of Developing Societies, New Delhi, Institute of Development Studies, Kolkata, Bangalore University, and Mahatma Gandhi University, Kottayam. All the chapters included in this monograph have been presented in those institutions in the academic programmes organized in the respective institutions. Hence, I express my sincere gratitude to those institutions and the organizers of these programmes. Finally, the fellow teachers in my department and the research assistants' who work with me deserve my appreciation. My family unit is always a part of my academic exercise and hence, I express my sincere thanks to my wife P. Mala.

G. Palanithurai

PERSONAL NOTE

I am writing this book based on my experience in working with communities and institutions as an academic activist in the past two decades with an aim of promoting equality and dignity for the poor and marginalized through the process of democratization and decentralization. This task I have chosen as an option to work with the poor and other marginalized groups as a professional imperative in higher learning institution under the pretext of outreach activities or extension programme. Although I kept a perspective that we have to work with them and not for them. In this process, I found enormous opportunities for the poor and the marginalized in decentralization for their emancipation and empowerment. If those opportunities and potentials are being used by the stakeholders, transformation is assured. Making use of this new opportunity is not so easy in Indian society as social forces and practices working in the society are antithetical to democracy. Wherever the poor and the marginalized are facilitated by either civil society organizations and academic institutions, transformations are visible. Equality and dignity have been achieved. But, these achievements are through a process of a prolonged struggle. It has been demonstrated that there is no short-cut and it is only through a process of struggle and for which democracy facilitates. The whole transformative process of the communities and groups has been captured in this book. While capturing the real life stories focus will be given as to what extent academicians can play an effective role in democracy promotion activities. This is captured with a view to demonstrate that the higher learning institutions can perform the third dimension of the academic activity, namely outreach or extension which is missing in Indian higher learning institutions. If higher learning institutions are involved in outreach activities communities around the institutions could be transformed easily. (For more details about our activities, *see* the website: www. rajivgandhichairgri.org).

Contents

1
Decentralization
Unused Potentials

Introduction

Twenty years have gone after the introduction of the 73rd Amendment to the Constitution of India to establish a stable rural local governance mechanism in India. But the conditions and trends in the whole governance process in the country in the context of globalization have prompted us to make a realistic evaluation of the efforts of both Central and State Governments in strengthening the local governance system in India and their impact on the transformative process of Indian society. Here, the assumption is that when globalization processes are on, it would not facilitate decentralization to gain strength to work for the poor instead it would facilitate decentralization to work for the market and the rich. Decentralization is being perceived as an instrument to facilitate globalization to move faster. It is the perception developed by one group of scholars in India. In the above backdrop local governance has to be evaluated in terms of its capacity to democracies, the communities and do service to the people to enable them to lead a decent human life with dignity. But, this task is not so easy as India being a vast country with vast and intensive differences and disparities in socio-economic conditions of the communities. Further, differences are many in governance and administrative pattern of the State

Governments in response to the demands of the people. Against this background a modest attempt is made to map up the efforts in strengthening Panchayati Raj system and its implications in the society.

Basics for Evaluation

The 73rd Amendment to the Constitution of India came into being with a set of goals.[1] They are: (a) working for economic development; (b) achieving social justice; (c) establishing a governance at the local level; (d) democratizing the community; (e) all the activities have to be carried out through a participatory process; and (f) establishing an inclusive governance and inclusive development process. Analysis of local government at the rural areas has to keep the above objectives in the backdrop. Based on the objectives the following questions are being raised here: (a) Has our Panchayati Raj system worked for economic development? (b) Has our rural local governance system worked for achieving social justice? (c) Has a governance system been established with independent powers to collect taxes and commit expenditures? (d) Has the new system of governance democratized the communities attitudinally and behaviourally through the conduct of meetings and discourses in the rural local bodies? (e) Has the system prepared a planning document with the vision and participation of the people? (f) Has the governance system created space for inclusion of women and *dalits* in governance and development process?

Perspectives

Perspectives vary from discipline to discipline. The subject decentralization has been studied by economist, sociologist, political scientist and others. All pan-India studies have been conducted by economist[2] barring one conducted by the Ministry of Panchayati Raj, Government of India.[3] The economists focus on only the fiscal federalism and revenue generation and expenditure of the local bodies. The economic studies further focus on service provision. Beyond the above they have no other concern. The Constitutional Amendment does not confine only the aspects of economic development. It goes beyond economic development. If touches upon social transformation and social justice through the involvement of stakeholders in the process of government and development. Of course scholars from other disciplines have covered many aspects of decentralization beyond its basic framework. The sociologists' focus is on the social transformation process initiated by the local bodies. Political scientists' focus is on governance, democratization and social justice activities of the local bodies. All these studies have adopted only conventional methodological nuances for data collection and data analysis. To study the local governance process in India lot more newer nuances are needed. While scanning the literature produced so far on local governance it is found out that a large number of problems have not been touched upon. So far very poor academic attention has been given on the issues of rural local governance. Till date hardcore academics are struggling to form an academy exclusively to focus on local governance issues in research. Journals are rare in this field. Government of India finds it difficult to find specialized institute to do research on core issues identified by the Ministry of Panchayati Raj.

Theory on Decentralization

Decentralization will be effective only if the region or state has higher literacy rate. In the same way the region should have the presence of politically enlightened citizenry, absence of high inequality in economic and social status that inhibits political participation of the poor, prevalence of law and order, conduct of free and fair elections, presence of strong civil society organizations, presence of active media, successful implementation of land reforms, adequate devolution of powers, capacitated local leaders, presence of strong will on the part of the state leaders and the vigilance of the public through awareness creation.[4] These factors are essential for the success of decentralization of powers. They are essential factors, but not the sufficient factors. Of the sufficient factors, leadership plays an important part. Hence, it is a new addition in the existing literature on decentralization. Leadership is the quality, capacity and character of an individual who is in the helm of affairs either in organization or institution or movement in tackling the issue through its attitude, behaviour and activities in the respective organization, institution and movement.

Methodology

This assessment and evaluation of decentralization process and its implications fully relied on the pan-Indian studies conducted by the World Bank, IDRC, Government of India and other agencies. Apart from the above state specific studies and regional studies conducted by various agencies over a period of time have been taken into account in this study. There are academics, policy-makers and a few bureaucrats who have been in the field for a period of thirty years. Their write ups, observations and presentations are taken into account for this evaluation. Reports of both Central and State Governments have been considered for this work. Author of this chapter being an academic activist participated in many of the State and Central Government committee meetings and through his participant observation, contribute substantially in the form of monographs, articles and books.[5] All the above documents have been used for this write up. All the studies have been referred from the perspective of the objectives and the questions raised in the above pages.

Major Observations

There is no evidence in the reports that the rural local bodies have worked for economic development. Of course, there are case studies established evidences that the panchayats have worked for economic development because of the leadership. There are substantial evidences to suggest that wherever expertise exist and where they are allowed to function have managed panchayats resources, education, waste and even to reduce vulnerability of households. Yet another issue relating to decentralization is law of subsidiarity one has to ponder over at this juncture. The key principle which is to be used for decentralization process is law of subsidiarity. But law of subsidiarity is totally missing in the process of decentralization in India. In the beginning of decentralization initiative it was in rhetoric high in order. But in reality one could not find any trace of it. While analyzing the decentralization process, it is found out that despite all the barriers, local bodies are delivering goods and services to the people. Having seen the dynamics there is no worthwhile policy note for rural development. Significant portion of achievements of local governance are attributed to the nature of leadership.[6] But it could not be confirmed through the pan-Indian studies. It needs deeper analysis and theorization. There was no concerted attempt on the part of Central and State Governments to enable the panchayats to work for economic development. Even in Kerala, there could not be any trace of economic development activities substantially. But evidences are there in Kerala that substantial amount of resources have been spent for poor.[7] Hence, one can argue that it worked for the poor. While making an analysis as to what extent the Kerala panchayats have achieved inclusive governance and inclusive development, it is learnt that it has helped partially the scheduled caste and it has not included the scheduled tribes. Despite all initiatives to strengthen local governance, the poor performance of the local bodies in attending to the issues of the ST would reflect the poor quality of governance.

It has been established through research that constitutionally mandated local governance system has been created in all the States. But it is only the creation of essential conditions for the establishment of the local governance system. To make the local governance system to work effectively and efficiently as autonomous governing system, sufficient conditions have to be created.[8] A sufficient condition implies the following things: (a) the representatives who are elected to institutions should have the needed capacity to handle and manage the institutions; (b) citizens should have adequate information and awareness about the responsibilities of these governance institutions and representatives; (c) power to hold the representatives of such institutions to account; and (d) financial autonomy in generating resources and to spend the resources to the local needs. In reality such sufficient conditions have not been created barring a few States to strengthen democratic decentralized local governance.

Simplified governance and administrative systems have to be in place. To handle the system and manage the process the elected representatives skills, capacity and capability have to be enhanced. To enable the citizens to participate in governance and development activities, needed awareness has to be created among the people about the new local governance process. To prepare a perspective plan with the participation of people a team of technical man power has to be in place. Proper sensitization of bureaucracy to work with the elected representatives of the people has to be done. All the above steps are needed to establish sufficient conditions for the smooth functioning of the rural local bodies. In reality they are not in place in most of the States.

Local bodies have been created and they have to function. As sufficient conditions have not been created, they have to face volley of problems in the development and governance process in the local bodies. By facing an array of obstacles, the local bodies have delivered services.[9] The rural local bodies have demonstrated that they have potentials and strength to carry the load of governance along with the State Government. Having understood the potentials[10] of the local bodies why State Governments are not strengthening the local governance system barring a few States is a question puzzling the research analysts.

It has been demonstrated that corruption in development sector in the rural areas has been reduced. But at the same time number of people involved in corruption has been increased. Through the establishment of local government machinery at the community level the gap between the government and the community has been reduced. Likewise information gap between the government and the people has been reduced. The cumbersome administrative process has facilitated the system to involve itself in corrupt practices. It is systemic in nature. In this corruptive process, benefits do not go to individuals but to system itself.

It is to be recognized that the Central institutions created at the dawn of Independence at the behest of Patel have not allowed the micro-institutions to grow and flourish in delivering services to the people. Much noise and voice were given at the dawn of Independence for establishing grassroots institutions for governance. But the context was favourable to the Centralized institutions for governance in the world. But now, the whole world has started moving towards decentralization. India ultimately moved closer to decentralization with a sense of commitment. Here, one has noted that by decentralization of powers the Central Government is not devolving its powers to State Government. Further, in the name of reforms to get advantage of globalization powers have been unrealized much against the wishes of the State Governments. That is why, it brought an amendment to the Constitution of India. By this process the Centre has compelled the States to devolve powers to local governments. By using this opportunity a few States made tremendous progress in establishing governance institutions at the grassroots. Having seen this achievement, many argue that India is missing a fine opportunity in bringing fundamental transformation in the society, governance and development.

Dalits have started asserting their positions and claiming their entitlements through local bodies. But they could not get the support base from Dalit organization working at State and National level. Likewise women have started asserting their positions and claiming their entitlements through local bodies. The Elected Women Representatives and the Elected Dalit Representatives have formed their own associations to redress their grievances. This does not mean that the elected women representatives and dalit representatives are free from obstacles and barriers.[11] The elected dalit representatives have been facing volley of problems in the community, polity and governance.[12]

Democratic decentralization stimulates increased political participation. It gives opportunity to ordinary poor citizens to influence decisions that affect their life. Information relating to governance, and development initiatives of the government has been flowing freely downwards. The flow is on both ways. Further, the democratic decentralization process integrates the governance and development institutions vertically and horizontally. It prompts the local council to act fastly and promptly. Local governments are acting as a link between the government and the people. Through local government, citizens and more particularly the poor have made both Central and State Governments accountable to them. Wherever informed leaderships are in the institutions, poor have secured more benefits and services.

It is found out that per capita bribe is more than the per capita tax. People have to pay more bribes for the services to be rendered by the Government Departments. This is because the local governance institutions have concentrated their attention more on service provisions rather than on governance. Further, even after the establishment of the local bodies, the development brokers continued to establish their sway over the delivery of benefits to the people and thereby they make money. That is why arguments are being projected that all services can be priced and they can be done professionally and people will pay for the services.

Throughout the country local body has been considered as an implementing agency of the Central and State Governments. The local body leaders have also perceived that they have to carry out the assigned roles in the local bodies.[13] Governance has been missed in the whole process of decentralization. Local bodies have to play an important role in creating database for the households of the concerned village panchayats for effective monitoring of the impact of all development activities and especially for poverty reduction activities. But unfortunately the local bodies are not equipped to generate, update and confirm the data base especially household data. Income generation through tax has not been improved. Unless tax collection is improved local bodies are only spending institutions. Sufficient tax base has to be created for local bodies. As of now, local bodies have not been given such responsibilities to strengthen the revenue base. There are potentials in local bodies to generate resources, but they are not allowed to generate resources.

Kerala is a model for operationalizing the 73rd Amendment to the Constitution of India, it has also several weaknesses. Even in Kerala benefits have not gone to the tribals. Kerala's own resource mobilization is also poor. Scheduled Caste has benefited to some extent. Pro-poor expenditure took place. Equally, synergy between self-help group (SHG) and Panchayat took place. Large number of good practices have taken place in the Panchayati Raj Institutions. Service delivery takes place effectively. Care and compassion services have taken place. It has not increased productivity and employment opportunities in the rural areas. Participatory planning has brought success and yet it could not move further. Proactive media, capacitated elected representatives, sensitized public have contributed substantially for the strengthening of the Panchayati Raj System. But officials' capacity has not been enhanced to the level of requirement of the society. In this process public institutions have been strengthened. Practice has been developed to work on the development needs of the community in Kerala.

Deliberative capacity and skill have been remarkably improved among the poor through their participation in Gram Sabha and Panchayat council meetings. The poor and ultra poor found potentials in Gram Sabha and they tried to fix panchayats accountable to them. They bring contestations, arguments, debates and discourse on development in Gram Sabha meetings. Gram Sabha acts as nursery for participatory democracy. It becomes a training institution for deliberative and participatory democracy. The following narratives will amplify the above observations:

NARRATIVE-I: DELIBERATIVE PROCESS

In a Gram Sabha meeting of a Gram Panchayat in Dindigul District (name of the Gram Panchayat is not disclosed deliberatively) the president of the Gram Panchayat opened the discussion by taking up the first item of the agenda. It is pertinent to solving an immediate problem faced by the people in the Panchayat. Since the Panchayat has got one and half lakh of rupees available at the disposal of the panchayat members of Gram Sabha evinced keen interest as decisions would be taken in the meeting itself and decision will be implemented immediately by the panchayats. The felt need of the people could be solved by using this amount. The moment the president opened this subject an old man stood up and informed the Gram Sabha that of all the problems people faced in this village, black top road is so important and essential for the new created colony. He continued his arguments. This is so important because in the past one year we have witnessed three matrimonial alliances about to be finalized for our village youth have not been settled as they have gone to other villages by indicating the fact that our village do not have good communication facilities for movements of cars and trucks. It is a shame on our part not to have such minimum facility. When all the villages have such facilities why we do not have such a facility? So roads, that too black top road, are the most essential need to finalize marriage alliance for our young girls and boys. He presented the matter in such a way that it would get the support of all. As soon as he completed his argument, an old lady made a plea that she needs a borewell in her residential area for drinking water supply. She argued that she is living in the outskirt of the main village and hence everyday women from that area have to come to the main village for fetching drinking water and when they come to main village for fetching drinking water, people those who are living in the main village objected the people coming from outside to fetch water from the main village. Hence, everyday they have to face such a problem and many of occasions they were ill treated by the people in the main village. She further explained that she belonged to *Dalit* community and hence coming to main village for fetching water creates lot of problem. It creates conflicts when people from *Dalit* community come to main village for fetching water. Many of the occasions it ended in manhandling. After her argument, the old man who demanded road for his new colony explained that there are pipelines up to the *Dalit* colony for water supply. Hence, the problem demanded by her does not arise. In response to the above argument the old lady argued that it is true that there is a pipeline, but water does not come through the pipeline. While distributing water, it starts from main village and the *Dalit* colony gets water at last. When it comes to its turn, water level goes down in the tank and there is no pressure in the tank. Hence, water supply is erratic. We made complaints many times to the Panchayat President. It is a well known fact to everybody and hence, she said that she brought to the notice of the Panchayat President. She asked the President of the Panchayat to explain to the people whether water comes through the pipeline or not. The Panchayat President informed the Gram Sabha that it is true that there is a pipeline, but water does not reach them as water availability does not permit us to allow the flow of water to many areas. Hence, we supply water to those areas very nearer to the main village. The President further informed that he has visited the place and know the conditions of these people. After the Presidents intervention, a few supported the argument of the old man's demand of a black top road. But nobody supported the cause of the poor women. Yet, the women stood up again and informed that she attended the gram sabha meeting not to bring an argument to develop debate over the issues. She came with the hope to make her case to prevail upon the members of Gram Sabha. Further, she told that she does not want to argue with anybody. She said, I left it here for a fair decision of the house (Gram Sabha). Having sensed the mood of the members, the Gram Panchayat President informed the Gram Sabha that both demands are genuine. Road is also necessary and equally water is also necessary. But availability of fund is limited. Hence, the Panchayat can take up only one. Of the two issues one can be taken up immediately. He said water is very essential and it is to be attended to. Road can be taken up later. In the same meeting a resolution can be passed that road work can be taken up next on a priority basis. With the available fund the Panchayat can take up now the water issue. He sought the cooperation of all. An old lady who was sitting by the side of the old man stood up and said that everyone has to agree to the proposal of Panchayat President. Since, there was no argument, the President thanked the members and went to the next item. Once the Gram Sabha meeting was over I went to the house of the *Dalit* women as I was witnessing the Gram Sabha proceedings with the permission of the Panchayat President. I asked the old woman, what made you to end the argument abruptly instead of continuing and left to the discretion of the President of the Panchayat? She informed me that she was interested only in getting her demand fulfilled and hence, she projected her plight and tried her level best to convince everyone. Further, she believed that the Panchayat leader who got convinced about her demand will play a fair role in deciding things. She further lamented that she developed a belief that mere arguments will not bring results the method of argument will make others to bring results. She further told me that the old man who was demanding a black top road, has constructed a new house for 80 lakh rupees in our village. He belongs to an upper class family. He has yet another old house in the main village. Since, his son is in the U.S.A. he has constructed a new house at a new place. Further, he has applied for a car loan to purchase a car and for which he needs a black top road. Since, he is a knowledgeable person, he put it in a logical and attractive way in the Gram Sabha meeting. It is a fact that everybody knows that he was demanding a black top road for his own sake. But nobody has opposed it as he belongs to an upper caste family. She told that she could have explained this fact in Gram Sabha meeting itself. But that would have created a communal clash and that is why she said, she could not bring that argument in Gram Sabha. Later I went to the old man's house to meet him. He was in his house. I initiated a talk pertinent to Gram Sabha. In this regard he said that he tried to convince everyone but failed. He further told that the Panchayat President has taken a decision in favour of *Dalits* as he relies on the vote bank of *Dalits*. While he was speaking to me, the old lady who was sitting by the side of the old man in *Gram Sabha* came from a room in the same house and told me that the decision of the Panchayat President was fair. Because the plight of women has to be redressed first, she said. Later I asked about her identity. She said that she came to Gram Sabha along with her husband who demanded a road. Here one has to understand the maturity of the *Dalit* women, Panchayat president and other old women in deliberating issues and taking decisions.

NARRATIVE-II: CREATION OF GROUND RULES

In Tamil Nadu, after the creation of New Panchayati Raj System by bringing conformity legislation, Gram Sabha was conducted. A photograph and write up about the Gram Sabha meeting with my observation was published in the Hindu daily. In the Gram Sabha meeting different types of chairs, benches have been used by different segments of the village community. A section of the community has been asked to stand. It was reported in the newspaper. It was explained as the social reality in the villages. It provoked the Government to create a ground rules for the conduct of Gram Sabha meeting. The State Government has prepared a ground rule for the conduct of Gram Sabha meeting in order to avoid exhibiting social hierarchy in seating arrangements in Gram Sabha, Government of Tamil Nadu has passed an order with needed details to make seating arrangements and how to conduct the Gram Sabha meeting without any discriminatory practices.

The next Gram Sabha meeting was conducted as per the instruction of the Government of Tamil Nadu. I went to a Gram Sabha meeting as an observer. Before I reached the venue of the Gram Sabha a young man came out from the meeting with clapping hands. I stopped him and asked him the reason for clapping while he is coming out from the meeting. He said Panchayat President told that the space created for everyone.

Everyone is equal in Gram Sabha. Hence, special seating arrangements have not been made. Everyone has to sit only on the floor and chair should not be used for Gram Sabha meeting. Hence, he was sitting in the Gram Sabha meeting by the side of the Traditional Panchayat leader. Since, untouchablity was practised in that village the young man who was sitting by the side of the Traditional Panchayat leader tried to touch him while sitting on the ground. He succeeded in his attempt in touching him. The moment he touched him, he felt that this act would infuriate him and hence, he thought that he has to leave the place. As a result, he came out from the meeting. After hearing the story from him I went to the Gram Sabha meeting. It went on for two hours. Once the meeting was over, I went to a tea stall and found double tumbler system. The officer who attended the Gram Sabha meeting on behalf of the District Administration told them that there should not be any discriminatory practice in this village. After the officer left the place, people who were in the tea stall observed that the Government Officer who came here as an observer on behalf of the District Administration may also be a Scheduled Caste person. As a result, the double tumbler system has been abolished after hearing from the Officer. People have been sensitized on the untouchability issue. From this event one has to infer that to remove untouchability Gram Sabha helps.

NARRATIVE-III: LEADERSHIP MATTERS MUCH

In yet another Gram Panchayat, three milch animals died after consuming polythene bags. The animals were owned by the poor SHG members of that village panchayat. The SHG members urged the Panchayat President to take steps to stop such occurrence in future. Initially, she was reluctant, but later she has agreed. While exploring the possibility, she found that the Gram Sabha is the suitable forum as it can decide on livelihood issues. She convened the meeting of Gram Sabha and in which the incidence was placed in one of the items for discussion. On the day of the Gram Sabha, the President requested the veterinary doctor to come and explain to the Gram Sabha members about the death of the above milch animals. He also came and explained to the people that the milch animals consumed the polythene bags and as a result all the three animals dead. Based on the explanation given by the Doctor people started the discussion and it continued for an hour. There were many suggestions offered and finally, they have arrived at a decision based on the discussions. They have decided unanimously that people should not use polythene bags in the villages of the panchayats. If they use it should not come to streets and public roads. People who violate the Gram Sabha resolution will be penalized. The responsibility of implementing the decision has been fixed on a person who is responsible for community affairs. It was implemented for about three months in the Panchayat area. As a result, the roads are clean and tidy. There is no polythene bag anywhere in the village. It became a clean village. This story was captured in a regional newspaper and as a result the District Collector visited the village and appreciated the President and he gave an award to the Panchayat in a meeting held in District Headquarters. The moment the incident was published in newspapers, a textile showroom from a nearby town has distributed a jute bag for every house as a compliment and it has to be used for carrying articles instead of polythene bags. It became a plastic and polythene free village. She became a role model for other Panchayat leaders.

NARRATIVE-IV: WHAT I GAINED THROUGH GRAM SABHA?

A Gram Sabha Member (Ms. Mariamma, 62 years old) in Karisalpatti Gram Panchayat in Dindigul District made an observation when our students are in the fieldwork. It is being reproduced here.

"Many of the government schemes are implemented by various departments and agencies in our village. Who is in which office, implemented the schemes of the government are not known to us. How to get such information is always a question like ring in my mind. When I heard that an observer is coming to Gram Sabha from the Government Department,

I thought that it is the best way to get such information from the Government Officer in Gram Sabha meeting. Hence, I have used Gram Sabha to track information. I have posited several questions about the details of the schemes, procedures of the schemes, operating officials and the location of the offices to the officer who came to Gram Sabha as an observer. I got all the information only from the Gram Sabha. This is possible because the observer coming from Government Department to Gram Sabha and explain to us. My close relative has not received old age pension for several months and she was not able to move out from her house. When it was raised in the Gram Sabha the Gram Panchayat President took responsibility to get details from the concerned office. Promptly the President took step to help the old woman. As a result, she got the pension. I am a wage earner in MGNREGA, and I was not sure of getting wages in time. Hence, I raised the question in the Gram Sabha. I got a detailed reply from the observer based on the Act. I am an unskilled labourer working in a farm. Panchayat operates drinking water supply regularly when I am in the farm. I raised it in the Gram Sabha. Since, many of the women belong to my street raised the same and the timing of drinking water supply has been changed to suit our requirement. When we raise question, we can get answer. Because Gram Sabha is a constitutional body and it has to be used. To me it is a Parliament. It is people's Parliament. If we know the powers of Gram Sabha, we can do many things for the poor. It is a poor people's institution. Originally, I got this information from our SHG meeting."

NARRATIVE-V: WHAT I GAINED THROUGH GRAM SABHA?

Mr. Muniasamy, a Gram Sabha member in Alamarathupatti Gram Panchayat in Dindigul District made an observation when our students went for a fieldwork. It is being reproduced here.

"Gram Sabha is a best place to demonstrate equality in an unequal society. Caste hierarchy is the reality in the rural areas.

Untouchability is yet another reality operates in different forms in the villages. Gram Sabha is an instrument to change the mindset of the people. A *dalit* cannot sit along with the higher caste persons in any social function in the village settings. But in Gram Sabha I find that equality at least in sitting along with them. I regularly attend the Gram Sabha meeting only to enjoy that equality in the village by sitting with higher caste men and women. Everybody has to sit only on the floor. Further, I can ask questions in the Gram Sabha. Questioning a higher caste person in a village is unacceptable. But in Gram Sabha being a President he or she has to respond to the questions of all. I raise many questions and I get answers to my questions. I enjoy questioning. I enjoy sitting with a higher caste person. It gives joy and happiness to me. Being a *dalit* I can only realize the joy."

NARRATIVE-VI: GRAM SABHA MEETING IN BOMMATHATHANUR

Bommathathanur village Panchayat is in Kelamangalam block of Krishnagiri district. It is a remote village having fifteen hamlets. It is a multi-caste and a bi-lingual village. There are nine ward members, six are male and three are female. SC and ST community have two ward members, one each and both of them are male members. There are four primary schools, one middle school and one high school in the Village Panchayat. For higher secondary education, students are going to Kelamangalam which is the block headquarters at a distance of 10 kilometres from the village Panchayat. Agriculture and animal husbandry are the major livelihood of the villagers. On the Independence Day 15.08.2014, Gram Sabha meeting was held in the village and its process is reported here. The Gram Sabha meeting was held at the premise of Ram temple located at the main village Bommathathanur. The meeting commenced at 11.00 a.m. The Panchayat President Smt. Mangamma presided over the meeting. The Panchayat Secretary welcomed the gathering and listed out the subjects in the agenda. From almost all hamlets villagers attended the meeting. There were 180 males and 140 females attended the meeting. It was noticed that elderly women and women members of SHG actively participated in the discussion. They fearlessly raised their questions. The participants from Scheduled Caste and Scheduled Tribes were encouraged to share their opinion by the Panchayat President. Major subjects which attracted the attention of the participants were drinking water supply, health and sanitation, Anganwadi Centre and school related issues, pension schemes under social security assistance, and the programmes of line departments implemented in the village Panchayat. Subjects like social audit of public distribution, Indira Awas Yojana, (IAY), Free Noon Meal Scheme in schools were also discussed during the Gram Sabha meeting. One participant who is a female aged 45 asked why there was delay in sinking of borewell for distribution of water to her hamlet. The President explained that the sinking of borewell was completed, but due to non-availability of adequate number of poles in the electricity department to bring electricity supply to the motor, so the project completion was delayed. He further told that the delay was reported to the higher officials of Electricity Board and assured the villagers that within two weeks period water supply would be commenced from the new borewell. One more subject in which participants showed interest was action taken to close the unused open well. The participants identified the open well and demanded to close it. But the President asked their opinion on the idea of instead of closing the open well permanently; it could be covered with the lid of iron as the water could be used during water scarcity. Many agreed for the suggestion of the President. In the subject of removal of poisonous parthenium weed plants, the President sought the cooperation and involvement of villagers along with youth and students who could remove all parthenium weed plants grown in the roadside and across the habitation. The President informed the participants that five solar lamps were sanctioned to the Panchayat main village and for four hamlets. On the subject of construction of household toilets, many participants informed that the cost of construction of toilet is always increasing. The Panchayat Secretary explained the provision in the MGNREGA work towards construction of toilets. 180 applicants are waiting to receive the subsidy cost and they requested the Government to act quickly so that they could commence the construction.

With respect of sub-standard work in the provision of cement concrete road, one participant raised the issue. At this juncture, the Union Councillor came forward and explained that due to non-availability of sand it was replaced with stone dust, the work was very bad. And it would be attended quickly and rectified. The President announced that two road works under Prime Minister Rozgar Yojana and NABARD assistance were sanctioned at the estimate of Rs. 89 lakh and Rs. 69 lakh and assumed that the quality monitoring would be ensured. Under Puthu Vazhvu Thittam, the SHG participants requested loan for purchase of goats to the eligible families. Villages demanded one Tamil medium primary school as there are around 25 Tamil speaking students who were facing difficulty in sustaining their education in Telugu language. The President told that the demand was already discussed in the earlier Gram Sabha meeting and the matter is in pursuance, the President added. In respect of protection of cattles from the seasonal disease Komari, the President informed that a medical camp for cattle was scheduled and requested the villagers to make use of the opportunity.

Social audit was conducted for Mid-Day Meal Schemes and IAY, but there was no noise. But social audit on Public Distribution Scheme (PDS) participants raised questions vociferously. They made complaints that the allocation of Kerosene oil to card holders is not adequate as it was reduced based on the assumption that the State Government gave the free supply of gas cylinder to card holders. But actually many families were left out. So, the villagers demanded to do resurvey on the number of card-holders who availed the free gas cylinder so that left out could get adequate Kerosene oil under PDS. Participants demanded to take efforts to bring public transportation facilities to students to go over to Kelamangalam Higher Secondary School to pursue their education.

A New Opportunity

The Fourteenth Finance Commission has submitted its reports and all the recommendations have been accepted by the Government. As a result, Rs. two lakh crore have been allocated for 2.5 lakh Gram Panchayats over a period of five years. On an average a Gram Panchayat would get Rs. 15 lakh every year. The amount goes to the Gram Panchayats. This amount can spent only on the core services of the local bodies. Only two mandatory conditions have been stipulated. Panchayats have to prepare perspective development plan and to conduct social audit. If they are fulfilled, the amount allocated will be given to the panchayats.[14] To help the Panchayats for the preparation of the development plan, all higher learning institutions have been instructed to work with communities through Unnath Bharat Abhiyan Scheme.[15] By using Fourteenth Finance Commission award and MGNREGA, Panchayat can be developed if State Governments take concerted effort.

At present 2.50 lakh institutions in the rural areas with 32 lakh elected representatives and of them 14 lakh representatives are women in the whole rural local body system in India. The number is not small. It is more than a critical mass. PESA is a powerful tool for the transformation of the ST. But in reality it has not helped the ST. It is not implemented. It is a sorry state of affairs. It is to be noted that increasingly the world is moving towards decentralization through reform process.[16] But in India, it is not moving forward. In the twenty years experience, it is proved beyond doubt that it produced unintended consequences. It has demonstrated its potentials. The whole world started believing the local governance to tackle the problems unsolved by the interventions of both Centre and State Governments. Efforts are on to find a meeting point between centralization and decentralization for establishing effective governance for delivering essential services to the people. Yet, it is not being strengthened. Why policy community is not evincing interest in strengthening the local body system despite the impact created by the local bodies on the life of the people in the rural areas.

In India, decentralization is a process of devolving powers from the State to local bodies and not from Central Government to State Governments and to local governments. By decentralization Centre wants to weaken the State. This is the perception of the State Governments. By creating local governments, State Governments respond to both the Centre and the local governments. Since, cooperative federalism is in practice there is no drive from the Central Government. It is the joint responsibility of both the Centre and State Governments to strengthen the local body system and to ensure delivery of services to the people. Now, under the new political regime the Central Government though abolished the Planning Commission at the Centre, it emphasized the need of the micro-plan at every village Panchayat. There is a hope that every Gram Panchayat has to prepare a perspective development plan to fulfil the obligations and equally it has to conduct social audit. Both for micro-plan and for conducting social audit, Panchayat needs professionals and the professionals have to be drawn from the higher learning academic institution under the scheme of Government of India (Unnath Bharat Abhiyan).

Conclusion

Initial years enthusiasm in decentralization of powers has been dwindled down now from among the policy community, and the donors as they feel there is no adequate drive from both the Central and State Governments to strengthen the local bodies despite they know that they have got huge potentials to serve the people and more specifically to the poor. A large number of donor agencies have withdrawn from funding local governance initiatives. As a result, many civil society organizations have withdrawn from working with local bodies. In the same way, many scholars who had evinced keen interest in local body issues in the initial years moved out of these issues in research. Local bodies have not emerged as institutions of governance. It has been perceived that the Central Government in the name of decentralization and strengthening local governance has started weakening the State Governments. In such a way definition for decentralization has been given. Decentralization in India essentially argues that power has to move from State Government to local governments not from Central Government to State Government. Local bodies have been looked at as institutions of spending and not doing the job of generating resources. The principle of subsidiarity is totally missing. One could notice several overlaps of functions among the tiers of local government. There is no worthwhile training policy to train the elected representatives of the people at the grassroots. Training institutions have not been properly shaped to train the leaders. There is no leadership school to shape transformational leaders at the rural local governance institutions. Cumbersome administrative process still continues to haunt the local body leaders. There is no administrative manual for local governance in many of the States. Till date, managing data pertinent to income and expenditure of the local bodies are problematic. The mandatory functions have not been carried out in the rural local bodies. Rural local bodies have not been enabled to perform the above mandatory functions. It has not generated the local resources and the rural local bodies have not been permitted to generate resources. Yet, it has created several unintended consequences. The Fourteenth Finance Commission through its recommendation has given a fresh impetus to local bodies functioning. How they are going to be used depends on the Centre and State Governments. The two decades experience amply demonstrates that decentralization of powers has got potentials to transform the communities. Even in a slow pace of decentralization, it has been noticed the assertion of *Dalits* and women and claims their entitlements. The potentials of decentralization have not been used.

NOTES

1. Government of India, 1994, *The 73rd Amendment to the Constitution of India,* New Delhi: Ministry of Rural Development.
2. Hari K. Nagarajan, Hans P. Binswanger Mkhize and S.S. Meenakshisundaram, 2015, *Decentralization and Empowerment for Rural Development,* New Delhi: Foundation Books.

3. Ministry of Panchayati Raj, 2008, *Study on Elected Women Representatives in Panchayati Raj Institutions,* New Delhi: Government of India.
4. Pranab Bardhan and Dilip Mookherjee (Eds.) 2007, *Decentralization and Local Governance in Developing Countries: A Comparative Perspective,* New Delhi: Oxford University Press.
5. Rajiv Gandhi Chair, 2007, *Ten Years of Decentralization Activities* Gandhigram: Rajiv Gandhi Chair for Panchayati Raj Studies.
6. G. Palanithurai, M.A. Thirunavukkarasu and G. Uma, 2008, *Change Makers at Grassroots,* New Delhi: Concept Publishing Company (P) Ltd.
7. S.M. Vijayanand, 2016, "Decentralization Experience in Kerala", Special lecture in the Thinkers Conference organized by Kerala Institute of Local Administration in Trissur, Kerala on 20th and 21st January.
8. James Manor, "Local Governance" in Niraja Gopal Jayal and Pratap Bhanu Mehta (eds.) 2011, *The Oxford Companion to Politics in India,* New Delhi: Oxford University Press.
   Government of India, 2015, *Fourteenth Finance Commission,* New Delhi: Ministry of Finance.
9. G. Palanithurai, 2012, *Elected Women Representatives and Empowerment,* New Delhi: Concept Publishing Company (P) Ltd.
10. Jean Paul Faguet, 2016, "Decentralization Promises and Performances" in the Thinkers Conference organized by Kerala Institute of Local Administration in Trissur, Kerala on 20th and 21st January.
11. Jean Paul Faguet and Caroline Posche (eds.), 2015, *Is Decentralization Good for Development? Perspectives from Academics and Policy-Makers* London: Oxford University Press.
12. G. Palanithurai, 2013, *Dalits and Dalit Representatives in Rural Local Governance: Voices from the Field,* New Delhi: Concept Publishing Company Pvt. Ltd.
13. Mani Shankar Aiyar, 2016, "In the Backdrop of Global Experience India's Experience in Decentralization", Special lecture in the Thinkers Conference organized by Kerala Institute of Local Administration in Trissur, Kerala on 20th and 21st January.
14. Government of India, 2015, *Guidelines for the Implementation of Recommendation of Fourteenth Finance Commission with regard to Local Bodies* No. 13 (32) FFC/FCD/2015-16, New Delhi: Ministry of Finance.
15. Government of India, *Unnath Bharat Abiyan* 2015, [F.No. 19-8/2014-TS-1 (sec)] New Delhi: Ministry of Human Resource Development.
16. James Manor, 1999, *The Political Economy of Democratic Decentralization* Washington DC: World Bank.
    Carl Wright, 2016, "Decentralization and Development: Experience from the Commonwealth Countries" in the Thinkers Conference organized by Kerala Institute of Local Administration in Trissur, Kerala on 20th and 21st January.

2

Democratization of Communities through Rural Local Governance

Introduction

In spite of its stability, democracy in India is in a nascent stage even after sixty-seven years of experience in practicing and upholding of the core values of democracy. The context and conditions with which democratic institutions started functioning prompted the scholars to be skeptical to its longevity. The functioning of the democratic institutions and practices of the core values of democracy may make one to observe that Indian democracy is still at minimum level. This evaluation is based on the practices of democracy in Indian polity and society as per the evaluative norms evolved to assess the democratic functioning, processes and procedures in any polity and society (Mair, 2008:108-132). It is a well known fact that in India all are equal politically, but not socially and economically. In the last six decades keeping India politically in electoral democracy in the backdrop of the presence of antithetical elements to democracy has been a herculean task (Weiner, 1989:21-23). People have been conscientized on the importance of suffrage and it did result in change of regimes. The changes in society towards democracy are slow, but transformational and yet Indian democracy could not move beyond electoral processes. Conducting election and allowing the elected to assume office without any disturbance are the two regular democratic activities continued since

Independence, except with a gap of two years during emergency. On all other core values of democracy, India is lagging behind many of the countries in the world. Yet many argue that even the survival of Indian democracy is through a hard struggle as it has to challenge many of anti-democratic social forces which are active in Indian society (Kumar, 1998: 3-23).

Since, Independence steps had been taken to democratise the communities through local governments, but this has not been as successful as expected because of the in-built weaknesses in the structure created for Democratization and development in the past (Narayan, 1964). In the new context, the historic amendment to the Constitution of India has opened up the Democratization processes and practices again on a sustainable basis. More specifically the 73rd Amendment to the Constitution of India, for first time introduced the democratic practices at the community level to take decision and implement the same collectively through a process of consociationalism by ensuring reservation of seats for the hitherto marginalized groups (Jayal, 2006: 1-26 and Singh, 2007: 1-36). In the given social context, it would bring many changes in the attitude and behaviour of the people at the grassroots when they are involved in collective decision-making in the new dispensation with the mandatory drawl of representatives from the *dalit* and marginalized groups (Manor, 2010: 61-79). Both conflict and harmony are the outcome of this decentralization processes and democratization at the community level (Palanithurai, 2014: 180-196). Since, the new dispensation involves decision-making, resource allocation as well as service provision it will pass through a process of struggle. It is to be noted here that the grassroots institutions are involved not only in achieving economic development and service provision, but also in administering social justice. The two governments above the local government have been struggling against the polarization of communities on the caste lines as engineered by the political class (Parekh, 2011). But this sensitive critical issue has been influencing the functioning of local bodies also

(Palanithurai, 2013). Twenty years have passed since, the establishment of the governance institutions at the community level based on the 73rd Amendment to the Constitution of India and India has witnessed both intended and unintended consequences of the significant Constitutional Amendment in the communities. Nature and intensity of the consequences have to be identified and evaluated. It is a massive task. Of all the implications and consequences of the historic amendment consequences in democratization of the communities is so important and vital for India. Hence, an attempt is made to evaluate to what extent the new dispensation has democratised the communities at the grassroots as it is a neglected area hitherto.

Justification for this Venture

There are studies evaluating the performance of the rural local bodies from the perspective of service provision and resource management by the economists (Nagarajan, Mkhize and Meenakshisundaram, 2015). There are studies evaluating activities carried out and initiatives taken by the rural local bodies by the political scientists and scholars of Public Administration (Ministry of Panchayati Raj, 2008). Of course, yet another set of studies conducted by the sociologists on the transformative process of the local bodies through governance and decision-making have emerged. Pan-Indian studies on rural local bodies are very few in number. Large number of studies are micro in nature. They have also significantly contributed in bringing new knowledge to the existing mass of knowledge on transformative process of the rural communities.[1] None has focused on the democratization process of the communities attempted through the rural local government institutions. In India all our focus is on the electoral process of the political system. Very rarely research ventures are attempted on the transformative process of the communities from the perspective of democratization of the communities. It is a gap in the existing body of knowledge on decentralization.

Broader Conceptualization

Before moving into the analysis of the issues involved, it is necessary to bring conceptual clarity on the concept of democracy. Till date there is no consensus on the meaning of the concept democracy (Crick, 2002). It is always remained a contested concept. Democracy in certain terms defies definition. Yet some broad contours are always on the discourse (Beachler, 1998). It is a set of institutions, processes and values involved in taking decisions on the life of the people who live in a defined territory. Its success depends on how effectively human collectivities handle those institutions and processes and adopt the values in their life. Democracy is not a law. It is an idea with potentials. Delivery of democracy depends on the average belief system and practices of the people on democracy. Democracy is a set of principles or doctrines of government; is a set of institutional arrangements and as a type of behaviour. All the above are in practice in the society with the participation of stakeholders. One cannot assume that they go together (Geddes, 1990). People have perceptions, understanding and knowledge about all and they act according to their level of understanding and interest. When democracy is practiced, one cannot expect that it is practiced as a conceptual entity, but it is based on their experience (Lijphart, 1989). People's perception and life conditions finally decide the course of action. The outcome of the people's participation will end in getting benefits for them and shaping the institutions of governance (Keefer, 2009). Level of participation depends on the level of benefits people get out of the governance institutions. People who get benefits will show respect to the institutions and the leaders who operate the institutions (McLaverty, 2011). People who could not get substantial benefits which they expect out of governance institutions will not respect the leaders and they will not evince interest and repose confidence in the institutions.

While looking at participation of people in the process of governance, one can easily come to a conclusion that despite poor delivery of the institutions, people who have no leisure will also evince keen interest in participating the institutions with a belief and confidence that they can fight for dignity, claims their entitlements and resist the oppressive culture in the society, provided the people are oriented in the democratization process (Dahl, 1972). The poor and the oppressed could see and believe that they can fight for decent life in the institutional set-up under democracy. Whether they are gaining material benefits substantially or not, they tend to evince interest to wage a war legitimately for equality and liberty on behalf of their communities (Vora and Palshikar, 2004). It tends to give a picture that the marginalized more specifically the oppressed and women have found enormous potentials to claim their dignity. Poor found that their problems could be solved through a process of negotiation. It is to be understood that this new form of democracy representative-*cum*-participatory democracy, interest of the individuals and groups will be negotiated through a process of governance as they get representation at all levels of governance institutions. Despite persisting poverty, illiteracy, inequality, deprivation, oppression, denigration, and indignation, people from lower segments continual to evince their interest in the present form of democracy (Kothari, 2005). It puzzles many. It raises many doubts (Marks and Dia, 1992). Yet, it is the reality (Mair, 2008). The reality is the hope with which they participate in the system despite several drawbacks for their participation. This kind of practice and perception of the people classify Indian democracy under substantive democracy. It essentially refers to the "existence of citizens as active agents capable of pursuing their interest with a measure of autonomy from entrenched structures of dominance and privilege" (Palanithurai, 2015). Against this backdrop an attempt is made to study the participation of women and *Dalit* members in the deliberative process of Gram Sabha and other grassroots institutions by adopting a case study method. The objective of the study is not to generalize, but to demonstrate the potentials of the institutions to democratize the communities on the core values of democracy.

Focus of the Study

This study tries to unearth the pain and pleasure of the women and other marginalized groups, while they try to participate in the governance process at the grassroots level along with other dominant caste groups. It tries to analyze to what extent the new initiatives for Democratization have created conflicts and harmony. Although the marginalized could raise only noise against the state when they are suppressed so far but now an opportunity has been created for transforming their noise into voice through Gram Sabha and Panchayat Councils. Now, a new narrative is emerging from the experience of the marginalized groups, while they participate in the process of governance and development at grassroots. The present study will highlight only such new narratives emerging out of a prolonged struggle against the dominant groups in the villages. They raise questions in the Panchayat Council and Gram Sabha, and the individuals who are in the helm of affairs never respect the dissent voice. In this context, the individuals who raised questions have to face several challenges. In the absence of clear cut ground rules for organizing meetings, the very meeting of Panchayat and Gram Sabhas are the expressions of dominance and establishment of superiority at the community level while it discharges its mandatory functions. The new narratives are drawn from various studies conducted in Tamil Nadu by the Rajiv Gandhi Chair for Panchayati Raj studies. These narratives will demonstrate the process of the struggle of the oppressed communities. It will capture the transformative process of the communities while they participate in Panchayat meeting and Gram Sabha meetings. This study will also analyze the deliberative structure and process of Gram Sabha meetings and their implications in the empowerment of the marginalized. From the narratives one could identify the possible hope for the marginalized to establish and enjoy equality at the grassroots.

Performance of the Rural Local Bodies

Before coming to the narrative of the experience of democratization, it is necessary to evaluate the impact of rural local governance on the rural communities as democratization acts both as ends and means. The new rural local bodies have brought intended and unintended consequences in the life of the people in the rural areas. In order to understand the process by which the poor and the marginalized and more particularly the women gain hope and faith in the governance institutions at the grassroots, it is necessary to understand the relationship between governance at grassroots and its implications in the life of the poor.

There is no evidence from the research reports so far produced that the rural local bodies have worked for economic development.[2] Of course, there are a few case studies established evidences that the panchayats have worked for economic development because of the leadership (Palanithurai, Thirunavukkarasu and Uma, 2008). There are substantial evidences to suggest that wherever expertise exist and where they are allowed panchayats can manage resources, education, waste and even to reduce vulnerability of households (Palanithurai, 2009). The key principle which is to be used for decentralization process is law of subsidiarity. But law of subsidiarity is totally missing in the process of decentralization in India. While analyzing the decentralization process, it is found out that despite all the barriers and obstacles, local bodies are delivering goods and services to the people. Having seen the dynamics there is no worthwhile policy note for rural development. Significant portion of achievements of local governance are attributed to the nature of leadership. But it could not be confirmed through the pan-Indian studies. It needs deeper analysis and theorization as leadership has got more scope for transforming the communities and societies (Denhardt and Denhardt, 2011). There are evidences to prove that in Kerala substantial amount of resources have been spent for poor. Hence, one can argue that it worked for the poor. While making an analysis as to what extent the Kerala panchayats have achieved inclusive governance and inclusive development, it is learnt that it has helped partially the Scheduled Caste and it has not included the Scheduled Tribes either in the process of development or in the process of governance. Despite all initiatives to strengthen local governance, the poor performance of the local bodies in attending to the issues of the ST would reflect the poor quality of governance.

By facing an array of obstacles, the local bodies have delivered services. The rural local bodies have demonstrated that they have potentials and strength to carry the load of governance along with the State Government. Having understood the potentials of the local bodies why State Governments are not strengthening the local governance system barring a few states is a question puzzling the researchers.[3]

It has been demonstrated that corruption in development sector in the rural areas has been reduced. But at the same time number of people involved in corruption has been increased. The cumbersome administrative process has facilitated the system to involve itself in corrupt practices. It is systematic in nature. In this corruptive process, benefits do not go to individuals, but to system itself. Through the establishment of local government machinery at the community level the gap between the government and the community has been reduced. Likewise information gap between the government and the people has been reduced.

A close observation of the ground reality reveals that the *dalits* have started asserting their positions and claiming their entitlements through local bodies. But they could not get the support base from *Dalit* organizations working at State and National level. Likewise women have started asserting their positions and claiming their entitlements through local bodies. They formed their own associations to redress their grievances. This does not mean that the elected women representatives are free from obstacles and barriers (Palanithurai, 2014). The elected *dalit* representatives have been facing volley of problems in the community, polity and governance.

Democratic decentralization stimulates increased political participation. It gives opportunity to ordinary poor citizens to influence decisions that affect their life. Information relating to governance, development initiatives of the government has been flowing freely downwards. The flow is on both ways. Further, the democratic decentralization process integrates the governance and development institutions vertically and horizontally. It prompts the local council to act fastly and promptly. Local governments are acting as a link between the government and the people. Through local government, citizens and more particularly the poor have made both Central and State Governments accountable to them. Wherever informed leaderships are in the institutions, poor have secured more benefits and services.

It is a common observation that per capita bribe is more than the per capita tax. People have to pay more bribes for the services to be rendered by the Government Departments. This is because the local governance institutions have concentrated their attention more on service provisions rather than on governance. Further, even after the establishment of the local bodies, the development brokers continued to establish their sway over the delivery of benefits to the people and thereby they make money. That is why arguments are being projected that all services can be priced and they can be done professionally and people will pay for the services.

Throughout the country local bodies have been considered as an implementing agency of the Central and State Governments. The local body leaders have also perceived that they have to carry out the assigned roles in the local bodies. Governance has been missed in the whole process of decentralization. Local bodies have to play an important role in creating database for the households of the concerned village panchayats for effective monitoring of the impact of all development activities and especially for poverty reduction activities. But unfortunately the local bodies are not equipped to generate, update and confirm the data base especially household data. Income generation through tax has not been improved. Unless tax collection is improved local bodies are only spending institutions. Sufficient tax base has to be created for local bodies. As of now local bodies have not been given such responsibilities to strengthen the revenue base. There are potentials in local bodies to generate resources but they are not allowed to generate resources.

Large numbers of good practice have taken place in the Panchayati Raj Institutions. Service delivery takes place effectively. Care and compassion services have taken place. It has not increased productivity and created employment opportunities in the rural areas. Participatory planning has brought success and yet it could not move further. Proactive media, capacitated elected representatives, sensitized public have contributed substantially for the strengthening of the Panchayati Raj system. But officials' capacity has not been enhanced to the level of requirements of the society. In this process public institutions have been strengthened. Practices have been developed to work on development needs of the community.

Deliberative capacity and skill have been remarkably improved among the poor through their participation in Gram Sabha and Panchayat Council meetings. The poor and ultra poor found potentials in Gram Sabha and they tried to fix panchayats accountable to them. They bring contestations, arguments, debates and discourse on development in Gram Sabha meetings. Gram Sabha acts as nursery for participatory democracy. It becomes a training institution for deliberative and participatory democracy. Democracy promotion activity can be engineered in local governance institutions. In local governance democracy promotion is integral part of it (Burnell, 2008). All the above observations are distilled from the research reports on decentralization in India. Most of the observations are drawn from pan-India studies conducted by bilateral and multilateral institutions. This will enable us to look at the democratization process perspectively.

Narratives on Democratization

Given below are the narrations of case studies observed in the field by the author as participant observation. They are taken from different periods. Since, the Rajiv Gandhi Chair has got an objective that it has to work for strengthening grassroots democracy, it prepared an administrative manual for rural local body administration. It has also prepared manual for the management of village panchayat, block panchayat and district panchayat. Apart from the above it prepared a guide book for the preparation of development plan for the village panchayat. It considers its seminal contribution in preparing the guide book for the conduct of Gram Sabha. It gives details of procedures for how to convene Gram Sabha, how to conduct Gram Sabha, how to pass resolution, how to discuss the items of agenda, how to record the resolutions, how to prepare agenda, how to make seating arrangement, how to allot time for each segment, how to listen the arguments, how to use language in the discussion and how to follow up the resolutions have been detailed in the guide book. Several thousand copies have been printed and circulated among the members of Gram Sabha with the support of civil society organizations. Subsequently, Government of Tamil Nadu asked the Rajiv Gandhi Chair to conduct a study on the functioning of Gram Sabha with an objective of strengthening Gram Sabha. Based on the report of the study series of steps had been taken to improve the functioning of Gram Sabha in Tamil Nadu. With the above background cases are narrated here under:

NARRATIVE-I: CREATION OF GROUND RULES

In Tamil Nadu, after the creation of New Panchayati Raj system, by bringing conformity legislation Gram Sabha was conducted. There was no clarity on the part of state administration as how to conduct Gram Sabha. After much pressure on the State Government by the civil society steps had been taken to convene Gram Sabha. First Gram Sabha meeting was convened in Tamil Nadu. It was a new experience for everyone. It was an excitement for everybody. This exercise was extensively reported in both English and vernacular newspaper. A photograph and write up about the Gram Sabha meeting with my observation was published in the *Hindu daily* and it provoked the government to create a ground rule for the conduct of Gram Sabha meeting. The State Government has prepared a ground rule for the conduct of Gram Sabha meeting in order to avoid exhibiting social hierarchy in seating arrangements in Gram Sabha, Government of Tamil Nadu has passed an order with needed details to make seating arrangements and how to conduct the Gram Sabha meeting without any discriminate practices.

The next Gram Sabha meeting was conducted as per the instruction of the Government of Tamil Nadu. I (author of this book) went to a Gram Sabha meeting as an observer. Before I reached the venue of the Gram Sabha a young man came out from the meeting with clapping hands. I stopped him and asked him the reason for clapping while he was coming out from the Gram Sabha meeting. He narrated what happened in Gram Sabha meeting. Panchayat President told that the space created for everyone. Everyone is equal in Gram Sabha. Hence, special seating arrangements have not been made. Everyone has to sit only on the floor and chair should not be used for Gram Sabha meeting. Thus, he was sitting in the Gram Sabha meeting by the side of the traditional Panchayat President. Since, untouchablity was practised in that village the young man tried to sit by the side of the traditional Panchayat leader and tried to touch him while sitting on the ground. He succeeded in his attempt in touching him. The moment he touched him, he felt that this act would infuriate him and hence, he thought that he has to leave the place. As a result, he came out from the meeting. After hearing the story from him, I went to the Gram Sabha meeting. It went on for two hours. Once, the meeting was over, I went to a tea stall and found the practice of double tumbler system in the tea stall. The officer who attended the Gram Sabha meeting on behalf of the district administration told them that there should not be any discriminatory practice in this village. After the officer left the place, people who were in the tea stall observed that the Government Officer who came here as an observer on behalf of the District Administration may also be a Scheduled Caste person. But, the owner of the tea shop was removing the glasses and put paper cups in that place. People have been sensitized on the untouchability issue. From this event one has to infer that to remove untouchability Gram Sabha helps. After a few days, the same boy was beaten up on some other pretext in the same village by a group of youth.

NARRATIVE-II: DELIBERATIVE PROCESS

In a Gram Sabha meeting of a Gram Panchayat in Dindigul District (name of the Gram Panchayat is not disclosed deliberately) the president of the Gram Panchayat opened the discussion by taking up the first item of the agenda. It is pertinent to solving an immediate problem faced by the people in the Panchayat. Since, the Panchayat has got one and half lakh of rupees available at the disposal of the panchayat. The felt need of the people could be solved by using this amount. The moment the President opened this subject an old man stood up and informed the Gram Sabha that of all the problems people faced in this village, black top road is so important and essential for a new by created colony. This is so important because in the past one year we have witnessed three matrimonial alliances about to be finalized for our village youth have not been settled as they have gone to other villages as they indicated our villages do not have good communication facilities for movements of cars and trucks. It is a shame on our part not to have such minimum facility. When all the villages have such facilities why we do not have such a facility? So, roads that too black top road are the most essential need to finalize marriage alliance for our young girls and boys. He presented the matter in such a way that it would get the support of all.

As soon as he completed his argument, an old lady made a plea that she needs a borewell in her residential area for drinking water supply. She argued that she is living in the outskirt of the main village and hence, everyday women from that area have to come to the main village for fetching drinking water and when they came to main village for fetching drinking water, people those who are living in the village objected the people coming from outside to fetch water from the main village. Hence, everyday they have to face such a problem and many of occasions they were ill treated by the people in the main village. She further explained that she belonged to *Dalit* community and hence coming to main village for fetching water creates lot of problem. It creates conflicts on *Dalit* community going over to main village for fetching water. Many of the occasions it ended in manhandling. After her argument, the old man who demanded road for his new colony explained that there are pipelines up to the *Dalit* colony. Hence, the problem demanded by her does not arise. In response to the above argument the old lady argued that it is true that there is a pipeline, but water does not come through the pipeline. While distributing water, it starts from main village and the *Dalit* colony gets water at least. When it comes to its turn, water level goes down in the tank and there is no pressure in tank. Hence, water supply is erratic. Complaints have been made many times to the Panchayat President. It is a well known fact to everybody and hence, she brought to the notice of the Panchayat President. She asked the president of the Panchayat to explain to the people whether water comes through the pipeline or not.

The Panchayat president informed the Gram Sabha that it is true that there is a pipeline but water does not reach them as water availability does not permit us to allow the flow of water to huge areas. Hence, we supply water to those areas very nearer to the main village. The President further informed that he has visited the place and know the conditions of these people. After the president intervention, a few supported the argument of the old man's demand of a black top road. But nobody supported the cause of the poor women. Yet the women stood up again and informed that she attended the Gram Sabha meeting not to bring argument to develop debate over the issues or to oppose any proposal. She came with the hope to make her case to prevail upon the members of Gram Sabha. Further told, she does not want to argue with anybody, I left it here for a fair decision of the house (Gram Sabha). Having sensed the mood of the members, the Gram Panchayat

President informed the Gram Sabha that both demands are genuine. Road is also necessary and equally water is also necessary. But availability of fund is limited. Hence, the Panchayat can take up only one. Of the two issues one can be taken up immediately. He said water is very essential and it is to be attended to. Road can be taken up later. In the same meeting a resolution can be passed that road work can be taken next on a priority basis. With the available fund the Panchayat can take up the water issue. He sought the cooperation of all. An old lady who was sitting by the side of the old man stood up and said that everyone has to agree to the proposal of Panchayat President. Since, there was no argument, the president thanked the members and went to the next item.

Once, the Gram Sabha meeting was over I went to the house of the *Dalit* women as I was witnessing the Gram Sabha proceedings with the permission of the Panchayat President. I asked the old women, what made you to end the argument abruptly instead of continuing and left to the discretion of the President of the Panchayat? She informed me that she was interested only in getting her demand fulfilled and hence, she projected her plight and tried her level best to convince everyone. Further, she believed that the Panchayat leader who got convinced about her demand will play a fair role in deciding things. She further lamented that she developed a belief that mere arguments will not bring results and the method of argument will make others to bring results. She further told me that the old man who was demanding a black top road, has constructed a new house for 80 lakh rupees in our village. He belongs to an upper class family. He has yet another old house in the main village. He has constructed a new house in a new place. Since, his son is in the US. Further he has applied for a car loan to purchase a car and for which he needs a black top road. Since, he is a knowledgeable person he put it in a logical and attractive way. It is a fact that everybody knows that he was demanding a black top road for his own sake. But nobody has opposed it as he belongs to an upper caste family. She told that she could have explained this fact in Gram Sabha meeting itself. But that would create a communal clash and that is why she said she could not bring that argument in Gram Sabha.

Later, I went to the old man's house to meet him. He was in his house. I initiated a talk with him pertinent to Gram Sabha held on that day. In this regard he said that he tried to convince everyone but failed. He further told that the Panchayat President has taken a decision in favour of *Dalits* as he relies on the vote bank of *Dalits*. While he was speaking to me the old lady who was sitting by the side of the old man in Gram Sabha came from a room in the same house and told me that the decision of the Panchayat President was fair. Because the plight of women has to be redressed first, she said. Later I asked about her identity. She said that she came to Gram Sabha along with her husband who demanded a road. Here, one has to understand the maturity of the *Dalit* women, Panchayat President and other old women in deliberating issues and taking decisions.

NARRATIVE-III: NEW RESPECT

Muthammal (name changed) was a maid servant working in a caste Hindu family to clean the cattle shed everyday. She has to clean the toilets along with the exterior space of the house. She has to remove cow dung from the cattle shed everyday. She will be provided old cooked food mostly rice and pickles for her breakfast. Later she has to go to farm work along with her husband. Both have to work in the farm owned by the same landlord. When the President post was reserved for *Dalit* women, a retired teacher from the *Dalit* community was promoted by a civil society organization to contest in the election. Muthammal's landlord asked Muthammal's husband to persuade Muthammal to contest in the election. Despite Muthammal resistance, she has been compelled to file her nomination. The landlord took it as a challenge and mobilized his caste people to defeat the retired teacher by giving a reason to the community that if she is elected, she will act independently and the social relation will be changed fastly and as a result our community's control over the *Dalits* will be eliminated. As a result without the effort of Muthammal, she was made to win the election. Till she was elected, she was confined to her house only. Muthammal has been asked by the District Collector to attend a training programme in a training institute. She attended the training programme. In the training programme the master trainers briefed about the transformation the Panchayat President has to achieve with the support of the communities in their areas. It was a transformational leadership programme. To bring such a transformation how the leaders have to change themselves attitudinally and behaviourally have been explained. Later Panchayat Administration was explained in the training programme. The whole training programme was an exercise for transformation. It was meant for fire creation. The moment she came from the training she went to panchayat office and sat in the panchayat office chair. First time in her life she sat in a chair in public office. It was a thrilling experience for her. She mentioned that she was in a different mood and perception. Later, she went to the house of the retired teacher who contested against her in the election and requested her to help her in managing panchayat by reading the administrative manual given to her during the training. She further asked her husband to stop going to the landlord house for farm work. Having seen the attitude of the Panchayat President the landlord has decided to sever his connection with this family. At this juncture, the landlord son from the US asked his father to construct a new villa in another place in the same village with a cost of 90 lakh rupees. It needs approval from the panchayat. Further, it requires road facility also for the new place and for which he requires the support of panchayats. One day the Panchayat President was standing on the road to supervise the MGNREGA works the landlord who passed by informed her that he will visit Panchayat Office to get her signature. She respectfully asked him the reason for his visit to Panchayat Office. He said that he has to get the approval from the panchayat for the construction of the new building. She said that she would come to his house to collect the paper and process the same in the office for according approval. She went to her landlord house and she was received by him and provided a seat to her inside the house. It was a new respect she got in the house. When this was narrated to her husband and son by her they could not believe it. She narrated this story in one of the refresher programme organized in a training programme. The author after hearing this story visited the landlord and asked about this transformation. He said that a *Dalit* uneducated lady showed such magnanimity and maturity in dealing with this issue, we have to show our maturity and we have to reciprocate and hence, I offered a seat in my house. Further, he informed that one has to understand the change that takes place in the society. Accordingly, he said that we have to change and transform ourselves. Our education has to help us to transform us. This was the last statement he made.

NARRATIVE-IV: LEADERSHIP MATTERS MUCH

In yet another Gram Panchayat, three milch animals died after consuming polythene bags. The animals were owned by the poor SHG members of that village panchayat. The SHG members urged the Panchayat President to take steps to stop such occurrence in future. Initially, the Panchayat President (women) was reluctant and later she has agreed. While exploring the possibility, she found that the Gram Sabha is the suitable forum as it can decide on livelihood issues and hence, it can be taken up. While interacting with her, she said that she tried to put it in Gram Sabha discussion not with the hope of solving the problem, but she felt that she has to respond to the call of the people. She wanted to be responsive and to some extent responsible at least morally if not legally. She convened the meeting of Gram Sabha and in which the incidence was placed in one of the items for discussion. On the day of the Gram Sabha, the President requested the veterinary Doctor to come and explain to the Gram Sabha members about the death of the above milch animals. In this context, she was very clear no discussion on mere assumptions, but it should be on a scientific basis. Hence, she called the veterinary Doctor. The Doctor also came and explained to the people that the milch animals consumed the polythene bags and as a result all the three animals dead. The Doctor issued a certificate based on his examination of the dead animals. Based on the explanation given by the Doctor people started the discussion and it continued for an hour. There were many suggestions offered and finally, they have arrived at a decision based on the discussions. They have decided unanimously that people should not use polythene bags in the villages of the panchayats. If they use it should not come to streets and public roads. It is their responsibility to manage it. People who violate the Gram Sabha resolution will be penalized. The responsibility of implementing the decision has been fixed on a person who is responsible for community affairs. In order to avoid legal complications the Panchayat Leader put the responsibility on the community leader. It was implemented for about three months in the Panchayat area. It was captured in a regional newspaper and as a result the District Collector visited the village and appreciated the president and he gave an award to the Panchayat in a meeting held in district headquarters. The moment the incident was published in newspapers, a textile showroom from a nearby town has distributed a jute bag for every house as a compliment and it has to be used for carrying articles instead of polythene bags. It became a plastic and polythene free village.

NARRATIVE-V: WHAT I GAINED THROUGH GRAM SABHA?

A Gram Sabha Member (Ms. Mariamma, 62 Years old) in Karisalpatti Gram Panchayat in Dindigul District made an observation when our students are in the fieldwork. It is being reproduced here. "Many of the government schemes are implemented by various departments and agencies in our village. Who is in which office, implemented the schemes of the government are not known to us. How to get such information is always a question like ring in my mind. When

I heard that an observer is coming to Gram Sabha from the Government Departments, I thought that it is the best way to get such information from the Government Officer in Gram Sabha meeting. Hence, I started attending Gram Sabha meeting and raised questions about schemes and programmes of the Government and I got reply from the observer. When I got needed information from Gram Sabha I developed a practice of attending Gram Sabha meeting to get information recognizing to development schemes and programme of the Government. Thus, I have used Gram Sabha to track information. I got all the information only from the Gram Sabha. This is possible because the observer coming from Government Department to Gram Sabha and explain to us. I moved further. To get benefit out of information we have to put demand in the Gram Sabha, because no other Sabha is nearer to me. Hence, I raised many issues in the Gram Sabha and made the President answerable and accountable to the people. My close relative has not received old age pension for several months and she was not able to move out from her house. When it was raised in the Gram Sabha the Gram Panchayat President took responsibility to get details from the concerned office. Promptly, the president took step to help the old woman. As a result, she got the pension. I know providing old age pension is not the duty of the village Panchayat, but I wanted this institution to take responsibility to make the government office work for the needy. I am a wage earner in MGNREGA, and I was not sure of getting wages in time. Hence, I raised this issue in the Gram Sabha. I got information, answer and assurance from the Panchayat President. In the same way, when I was not able to get drinking water. I raised this issue in the Gram Sabha meeting. I got reply. I got regular water supply. I am an unskilled labourer working in a farm. Panchayat operates drinking water supply when I am in the farm. I raised it in the Gram Sabha. Since, many of the women belong to my street raised the same the timing of drinking water supply, it has been changed to suit our requirement. To me it is a parliament. I got this information from our SHG meeting."

NARRATIVE-VI: WHAT I GAINED THROUGH GRAM SABHA?

Mr. Muniasamy, a Gram Sabha member in Alamarathupatti Gram Panchayat in Dindigul District made an observation when our students went for a fieldwork. It is being reproduced here: "Gram Sabha is a best place to demonstrate equality in an unequal society. Caste hierarchy is the reality in the rural areas. Untouchability is yet another reality operates in different forms in the villages. Gram Sabha is an instrument to change the mindset of the people. A *Dalit* cannot sit along with the higher caste persons in any social function in the village settings. But in Gram Sabha I find that equality at least in sitting along with them. I regularly attend the Gram Sabha meeting only to enjoy that equality in the village by sitting with higher caste men and women. Everybody has to sit only on the floor. Further, I can ask questions in the Gram Sabha. Questioning a higher caste person in a village is unacceptable. But in Gram Sabha being a President, he or she, has to respond to the questions of all. I raise many questions and I get answers to my questions. I enjoy questioning. I enjoy sitting with a higher caste person. It gives joy and happiness. Being a *dalit* I can only realize the joy."

NARRATIVE-VII: RULES FOR MEETING AND DISCUSSION

Rani Sathappan, K. Rayavaram Gram Panchayat, Pudukkottai district set a standard for meeting of Panchayats and Gram Sabhas. In every meeting opportunity is being given to all and equal time is allotted for their participation. No one is allowed to leave the meeting in the middle after speaking their points. They have to speak and listen also. Every decision was taken on a consensus basis not on majority. She stipulated that no one use unparliamentary words in the discussion. She allowed Gram Sabha members as visitors to sit in Panchayat Council meeting. She conducted all the committee meetings of the Gram Panchayats. In the five years tenure, she concentrated much on evolving a deliberative and discourse culture. When she participated in the annual meeting of the Federation of Elected Women representatives of Tamil Nadu, she was appreciated by all and more especially by the then Director of Rural Development and the then District Collector of Dindigul. She evolved the consensual decision-making process only through persuasion. She has developed this approach only by evolving a strategy of working collectively and transparently. She first created an image for her as honest Panchayat President. Her integrity and sobriety made her to gain a good leadership image among the people.

NARRATIVE-VIII: GRAM SABHA MEETING IN BOMMATHATHANUR

Bommathathanur village Panchayat is in Kelamangalam Block of Krishnagiri district. It is a remote village having fifteen hamlets. It is a multi-caste and a bi-lingual village. There are nine ward members, six are male and three are female. SC and ST community has ward member, one each and both of them are male members. There are four primary schools, one middle school and one high school in the Village Panchayat. For higher secondary education, students are going to Kelamangalam which is the block headquarters at a distance of 10 kilometres from the village Panchayat. Agriculture and animal husbandry are the major livelihood of the villagers. The villagers and the elected representatives are active in CFVP of UNICEF. On the Independence Day 15.08.2014 Gram Sabha meeting was held in the village and its process is reported here. The Gram Sabha meeting was held at the premise of Ram temple located at the main village Bommathathanur. The meeting commenced at 11.00 a.m. The Panchayat President Smt. Mangamma presided over the meeting. The Panchayat Secretary welcomed the gathering and listed out the subjects in the agenda. From almost all hamlets villagers attended the meeting. There were 180 males and 140 females attending the meeting. It is noticed that elderly women and women members of SHG actively participated in the discussion. They fearlessly raised their questions. The participants from Scheduled Castes and Scheduled Tribes were encouraged to share their opinion by the Panchayat President. Major subjects which attracted the attention of the participants were drinking water supply, health and sanitation, Anganwadi centre and school related issues, pension schemes under social security assistance, and the programmes of line departments implemented in the village Panchayat. Subjects like social audit of public distribution, Indira Awas Yojana, Mid-Day meal scheme in schools were also discussed during the Gram Sabha meeting. One participant who is a female aged 45 asked why there was delay in sinking of borewell for distribution of water to her hamlet. The President explained that the sinking of borewell was completed, but due to non-availability of adequate number of poles in the Electricity Department to bring electricity supply to the motor the projectcompletion was delayed. He further told that the delay was reported to the higher officials of Electricity Board and assured the villagers that within two weeks period water supply would be distributed from the new borewell. One more subject in which participants showed interest was action taken to close the unused open well. The participants identified the open well and demanded to close it. But the President asked their opinion on the idea of instead of closing the open well permanently; it could be covered with the bid of iron as the water could be used during water scarcity. Many agreed for the suggestion of the President. In the subject of removal of poisonous parthenium weed plants, the President sought the cooperation and involvement of villagers along with youth and students who could remove all parthenium weed plants grown in the roadside and across the habitation. The President informed the participants that five solar lamps were sanctioned to the Panchayat main village and for four hamlets. On the subject of construction of household toilets, many participants informed that the cost of construction of toilet is always increasing. The Panchayat secretary explained the provision in the MGNREGA work towards construction of toilets. 180 applicants are waiting to receive the subsidy cost and they requested the Government to act quickly so that they could commence the construction.

With respect of sub-standard work in the provision of cement concrete road, one participant raised the issue. At this juncture, the Union Councillor came forward and explained that due to non-availability of sand which was replaced with stone dust the work was very bad. And it would be attended quickly and rectified. The President announced that two road works under Prime Minister Rozgar Yojana and NABARD assistance were sanctioned at the estimate of Rs. 89 lakh and Rs. 69 lakh and assumed that the quality monitoring would be ensured. Under Puthu Vazhvu Thittam, the SHG participants requested loan for purchase of goats to the eligible families. Villages demanded one Tamil medium primary school as there are around 25 Tamil speaking students who were facing difficulty in sustaining their education in Telugu language. The President told that the demand was already discussed in the earlier Gram Sabha meeting and the matter is in pursuance, the President added. In respect of protection of cattles from the seasonal disease Komari, the President informed that a medical camp for cattle was scheduled and requested the villagers to make use of the opportunity.

Social audit was conducted for Mid-Day Meal Schemes and IAY, but there was no noise. But social audit on PDS participants raised questions vociferously. They made complaints that the allocation of Kerosene oil to card holders is not adequate as it was reduced based on the assumption that the State Government gave the free supply of gas cylinder to card holders. But actually many families were left out. So, the villagers demanded to do resurvey on the number of card-holders who availed the free gas cylinder so that left out could get adequate kerosene oil under PDS. Participants demanded to take efforts to bring public transportation facilities to students to go over to Kelamangalam higher secondary school to pursue their education.

Interpretation and Explanation

From the narratives the following conjunctures are derived:

A mere ground rules for the conduct of the Gram Sabha created an opportunity to the marginalized and excluded to enjoy equality by acquiring place and seat along with the dominant groups which itself is considered as an achievement by the oppressed. It enables them to speak out their grievances and to reduce the asymmetry of information on the development schemes and programmes for the poor. By mere getting the information openly in the Gram Sabha, the depressed are giving the messages that they are aware of the laws on against discriminatory practices. This paved the way for slow transformation in the social practices of the communities. But this transformation was not smooth. It is a process of struggle.

When a leader facilitated a discourse in a Gram Sabha in an enlightened way, a woman from an oppressed community through a process of argumentative ability to convince a crowd drawn from different socio-economic sector to get justice for the poor from the oppressed community. It raises hope that by raising issues by adopting a strategy one can prevail upon the community to take call for the plight of the oppressed. Democracy has to be visualized in such a way and evolve strategy to communicate their plight in a convincing way without antagonizing the others. Discourse ability will turn the group towards fairness and justice. The need of the hour is negotiating skill and communication skill.

By acquiring skill, capacity and commitment one can manage governance provided the leader should have ability to negotiate with the dominant class. The ability to negotiate with the dominant class lies with the leader in exhibiting the governance skill and maturity in maintaining interpersonal relations. Empowerment and leadership quality gives maturity to manage the institutions and by which one can get recognition and respect. In this process democracy provides opportunity for the dominant class to understand the process of emancipation and empowerment of the depressed. Since, dominant classes are in the path of consolidating their economic position, they tend to change their strategies to work with the depressed in harmony.

Finest and consensus decisions could be evolved through a passionate, intense and committed discourse through the involvement of all segments of the society with a hope to everyone that the leadership will act fairly and judiciously. A democratic leadership alone will enable a passionate discourse in the Gram Sabha by creating a hope that the institution will work for the common good.

When leadership raises hope among the poor that the democratic institutions provide opportunity to gain information and use information to solve their problems, people will evince interest in participating in the deliberations of democratic institutions. Democracy is not mere debate and discourse, but it should lead to fair decision. If such a condition is created, people whether they find leisure or not, they will participate in the deliberations.

Further, it provides opportunity to ventilate the grievances of the voiceless in the public deliberations with a proper moderation will eliminate the frustrations of the voiceless. The decentralized democratic practices will ease the frustrations of the poor. This process of raising question and the process of listening and respecting the questions are the real game changers in transforming the individual. It requires a consensual and matured democratic leader.

Gram Sabha should not end with mere passing of resolution based on the discussion. It has to deliver goods to the people. When such a kind of institutional mechanism is in place, it has got the tremendous potentials to bring transformation in the communities. It needs democratic leader. Such leaders can be moulded and shaped through a democratic training process. It is not an administrative training. It is training for democratic transformation at the grassroots.

From the narratives one can easily infer the potential of democracy to bring change in the attitude and behaviour of the people. It will move from procedural to substantive democracy. In our local bodies much attention was given only on implementing the schemes and programmes of both the Centre and the State Governments. Service provision was considered as most essential responsibility of the panchayats. Panchayats are monitored and evaluated from the perspective of implementing schemes and programmes and not from the perspective of democratic governance. As a result, governance is missing in our rural local bodies. Though, the Constitutional Amendment and Confirmative Act of the state emphasize the need of the stakeholder's participation, it is not found in the core of evaluation. Hence, it loses its importance. But, wherever leaders are shaped and moulded through a training process those leaders play a remarkable role in transforming themselves and transforming the communities interms of the attitude and behaviour of the people towards democratization. Democracy promotion takes place at the Panchayat level and community level. But it requires enabling conditions. Democratization was not given that much of importance in the mainstream discourse on decentralization. Wherever the Panchayat Presidents are trained and oriented as transformational leaders, there one could witness the transformation through the use of democratization while discharging their functions. Basically, it relies on the leaders. Leadership has got a role to play in managing institutions and transforming the communities through democratization. It requires maturity on the part of the leaders. It comes through a process of widening their vision and connections. The leaders have to enable the participants of the assemblies, councils, Sabhas and committees to enjoy the power of argument, discussion, discourse and debates. When they start enjoying arguments and debates, everyone will evince in passionate discourses. This process will ensure equality, respect others, respect dissent voice, exhibiting fairness, and justice. It will enable the people to exhibit maturity and magnanimity on a competitive basis. The pleasure of the leadership lies not in carrying and executing volume of works by spending millions of rupees, but, it lies in how the whole panchayat activities are being carried out collectively. Leadership lies in bringing passion among people to develop arguments and arrive decisions on consensus basis. When opportunities are created for the people to raise questions, many enjoy questioning authority. Whether they get sufficient answer to solve their problems or not, they enjoy questioning. This democratization process will ease out tension and frustration of the people. They have forum and responsible people to listen to their arguments and problems and this enable them to ventilate their emotions and tensions. Stakeholders use democracy as a tool to achieve their end. This democratization process comes at point where retreat of democracy started at a higher level because of globalization of economy (Basu, 2007). Contextualization, renewal and rejuvenation of democracy is needed at all levels all over the world (Ginsborg, 2009). They need service, they need goods and they use democratic processes to achieve the above. To do the above leadership plays a crucial role. To achieve such a kind of leadership, training played a key and pivotal role. In the training modules of the training institution in India one could not see the aspect of democratization of the communities. Deepening of democracy has to take place only through the rural local bodies. Unfortunately in the training programme, this is a missing element. All our institutions at the ground are to practice democracy in their functioning. The leaders have to enable the people to make use of the opportunity to develop a democratic culture through a participatory, argumentative consensual decision-making process.

Conclusion

In the whole twenty years of democratic decentralization process, democratization has been a missing element and it has not received the needed attention from both the Central and State Governments. It has been left out even in the capacity-building exercises of the training institutions. There are a few institutions which concentrate on this issue in training. Well-meaning and committed leaders have understood the potentials of democracy and used it to bring joy among the participants in evolving debates, discourses and discussions in Panchayat Council and Gram Sabha meetings. Extraordinarily, they transformed themselves as transformational leaders and transformed the communities. This kind of practices at the Gram Panchayat level demonstrate that the procedural democracy moves towards substantive democracy. It not only serves for strengthening of democratic process, but also to solve many of the socio-economic problems at the community level by evolving decisions on a consensus basis through the participation of stakeholders. The rich potentials are not used at the ground by both the Central and State Governments to solve the problems of deficit democracy through the effective democratic functioning of the local body institutions core values of democracy could be injected into the minds of the people. It brings changes in the attitude and behaviour of the stakeholders who participate in Gram Sabha and Panchayat meetings. From the narratives it has been demonstrated that democratization of institutions would bring a sea change in the attitude and behaviour of the people. It needs only a leadership and that too a transformational leadership. At present, we have only deficit of leadership. The deficit of leadership can be solved by evolving a training policy to conduct training programme on democratization for the rural local body leaders. Even higher learning academic and research institutions can work on democracy promotion activities through local bodies.

NOTES

1. James Manor has touched on those studies in his article on 'Local Governance', 2010.
2. S.M. Vijayanand, 2016, Secretary, Ministry of Panchayati Raj, Government of India has indicated this outcome of local governance in the Thinkers Conference organized in Kerala Institute of Local Administration, Trissur on 20th January.
3. James Manor and Hans P. Binswanger Mkhize have been raising this question every conference in front of the policy community.

REFERENCES

Basu, Kaushik (2007), *The Retreat of Democracy*, Ranikhet: Permanent Black.

Beachler, Jean (1998), *Democracy: An Analytical Survey*, New Delhi: National Book Trust.

Burnell, Peter (2008), "Promoting Democracy" in Daniele Caramani (ed.) *Comparative Politics*, New Delhi: Oxford University Press.

Crick, Bernard (2002), *Democracy: A Very Short Introduction*, New Delhi: Oxford University Press.

Dahl, Robert A., (1972), *Authority in a Good Society: After the Revolution?* New Delhi: Allied Publishers Private Limited.

Denhardt, Janet V., and Denhardt, Robert (2011), "Leadership" in Bevir, Mark (ed.) *The Sage Handbook of Governance*, New Delhi: Sage Publications.

Ginsborg, Paul (2009), *Democracy: Crisis and Renewal*, London: Profile Books Ltd.

Geddes, Barabara (2009), "What Causes Democratization?" in Charles Boix and Susan C. Stokes (eds.), *The Oxford Handbook of Comparative Politics*, New Delhi: Oxford University Press.

Jayal, Niraja Gopal (2006), "Introduction" in Jayal, Niraja Gopal, Prakash, Amit and Sharma, Pradeep K. (eds.), *Local Governance in India: Decentralization and Beyond*, New Delhi: Oxford University Press.

Keefer, Philip (2009), "The Poor Performance of Poor Democracies" in Charles Boix and Susan C. Stokes (eds.) *The Oxford Handbook of Comparative Politics*, New Delhi: Oxford University Press.

Kumar, Ravinder (1998), "Democracy: From Consolidation to Fluidity" in Karlekar, Hiranmay (ed.), *Independent India: The Finest Fifty Years*, New Delhi: Oxford University Press.

Kothari, Rajani (2005), *Rethinking Democracy*, Hyderabad: Orient Longman.

Lijphart, Arend (1989,) *Democracy in Plural Societies: A Comparative Exploration*, Bombay: Popular Prakashan.

Manor, James (2010), "Local Governance" in Jayal, Niraja Gopal and Mehta Pratap Bhanu (eds.) *The Oxford Companion to Politics in India*, New Delhi: Oxford University Press.

Marks, Gray and Dia Mond Larry (eds.), (1992), *Reexamining Democracy*, New Delhi: Sage Publications.

Mair, Peter (2008), "Democracies" in Daniele Caramani (ed.) *Comparative Politics*, New Delhi: Oxford University Press.

McLaverty, Peter (2011), "Participation" in Bevir, Mark (ed.) *The Sage Handbook of Governance*, New Delhi: Sage Publications.

Ministry of Panchayati Raj (2008), *Study on Elected Women Representatives in Panchayati Raj Institutions*, New Delhi: Government of India.

Narayan, Jayaprakash (1964) "Presidential Speech" in All India Panchayat Parishad, *Panchayati Raj: Perspective and Programme*, New Delhi: All India Panchayat Parishad.

Nagarajan, Hari K., Mkhize, Hans P. Binswanger and Meenakshisundaram, S.S. (2015), *Decentralization and Empowerment for Rural Development*, New Delhi: Foundation Books.

Palanithurai, G. (2013), *Dalits and Dalit Representatives in Rural Local Governance: Voices from the Field,* New Delhi: Concept Publishing Company (P) Ltd.

Palanithurai, G. (2015), *Deliberative Democracy,* New Delhi: MJP Publishers.

Palanithurai, G. (2009), *Panchayat in Disaster Preparedness and Management,* New Delhi: Concept Publishing Company (P) Ltd.

Palanithurai, G. (2014), *Governance Issues in India: From Grassroots Perspective,* New Delhi: Concept Publishing Company (P) Ltd.

Palanithurai, G. (ed.) (2014), *Federating Elected Women Representatives of Local Bodies in India,* New Delhi: Concept Publishing Company (P) Ltd.

Palanithurai, G., Thirunavukkarasu, M.A. and Uma, G. (eds.) (2008), *Change Makers at Grassroots,* New Delhi: Concept Publishing Company (P) Ltd.

Parekh, Bhikhu (2011), "The Crisis in Indian Democracy", Jawaharlal Nehru Memorial Lecture delivered in Trinity College on 21st November.

Singh, Satyajit (2007), "Introduction" in Singh, Satyajit and Sharma Pradeep K. (eds.), *Decentralization: Institutions and Politics in Rural India,* New Delhi: Oxford University Press.

Tata Institute of Social Sciences (2015), *Devolution Report 2014-15: How Effective in Devolution Across Indian States Insights from the Field,* New Delhi: Ministry of Panchayati Raj, Government of India.

Vora, Rajendra and Suhas Palshikar (eds.) (2004), *Indian Democracy Meanings and Practices,* New Delhi: Sage Publications.

Weiner, Myron (1989), *The Indian Paradox: Essays in Indian Politics,* New Delhi: Sage Publications.

3

Democracy Promotion through Decentralization of Powers in India

Introduction

Indian democracy is being viewed with much appreciation by the scholars in the West who specialize in democracy promotion because of the struggle it undergoes for sustaining the minimum values of democracy through the electoral process. This appreciation is not because of the quality of democracy that India maintains. It is because India maintains a minimal form of representative democracy continuously with a break of two years despite the play of an array of negative socio-political forces and practices against democracy.[1] Maintaining a minimum set of democratic values in India is not a simple task as India has more anti-democratic social practices which are vibrant and active in all spheres and activities of the communities in India.[2] It is an irony that even in political parties one could not see the healthy democratic practices despite the stipulation imposed by the Election Commission of India. Only a few political parties are practicing democratic values in their functioning. Many, in fact, wanted to evade from these practices. Even after sixty seven years of democratic practice, we are in minimal democracy[3] as per the standardized classification done by the scholars and we are in institutional democracy. Democracy is always in dynamic form and it evolves in different pattern in the world.[4] Tokenism and symbols are visible. In India the struggle is to transform the institutional democracy into a behavioural democracy by changing the attitude, belief, and behavioural traits of the people towards the values, and norms of democracy. The core values, namely the equality, liberty, freedom, justice, fairness, equity, respecting the dissent voice are not in social and political practices.[5] Having understood the nature and structure of Indian society, M.K. Gandhi rejected the adoption of Western model of representative democracy for governing the Indian society. He anticipated that this institution will be used to exploit the people by a few who are able to sneak into the governing system.[6] Hence, he outrighty rejected the Western model despite the whole hearted support extended to this model by a dominant segment in the intellectual group among the founding fathers of modern India. Yet, it has been adopted as creating centralized nation-state was the option of many of the liberated societies from the colonial yoke after the Second World War. When the whole world was moving towards centralized state system M.K. Gandhi advocated a decentralized governing system with the active participation of the people. It is also an irony that the intellectuals of the world took nearly forty years to realize the potentials of decentralization. Only after the four decades experience in democratic governance, many of the governments felt that the big government approach has not delivered the public goods effectively and the world has to move towards an alternative governance system to meet the unmet demands of the people.[7] In that context, 'decentralization' was considered as the best option to manage the resentment of the people over the poor performance of the state.[8] India is one among sixty countries entered into a big pang approach. India opted the path of constitutionalizing the process of decentralization and it has to move in a different path of democratization.[9]

Context

First time in Indian democratic governance history, a vibrant participatory local governance mechanism has been created through an Amendment to the Constitution of India. It is historic and pathbreaking in terms of its potentials to bring revolutionary changes in the socio-political and economic life of the poor and the marginalized provided the potentials are being understood by the stakeholders who are going to get benefits out it. The whole process of transformation would take place only through a democratic process. The decentralization process and democratization process are complementary to each other.[10] The two processes require enormous input from various segments of the society to produce intended results. Because what have not been achieved in the past through big government approach have been fixed as basic objectives of the new dispensation. The 73rd Amendment to the Constitution of India has promised economic development and social justice to the poor and marginalized. It will be achieved through a participatory democratic process with the involvement of the stakeholders in the process of governance and development. The above objectives appear to be simple, but to realize the same a mass movement is necessary and, unless otherwise, a mass movement is in place it is only rhetoric and not a reality. Even after twenty years of the practice of new local governance system in India, many are in search of reasons for the slowdown of interest in decentralization at present. But Jayaprakash Narayan made a pathbreaking analysis in his address in the Annual Conference of All India Panchayat Parishad Conference in Bangalore after demise of Nehru on the obstacles for decentralization of powers.[11] In this chapter what I intend to do is to investigate as to what extent the decentralization process has been achieved through a democratic process by leaving out the analysis of the impact of decentralization in the communities at the grassroots. While doing so I will highlight what a higher learning institution can do for democracy promotion and deepening activities through the experience of a Department in a small university.

Challenges

Decentralization and democratization in a society which is diverse in character and known for its inequality and inequity have to face challenges and stiff resistance. Both provide opportunities to the hitherto marginalized and excluded communities and groups to participate in the process of governance and development. If both are understood broadly and perspectively one will find the potentials to bring fundamental change at the community level. It requires a thorough preparation and massive mobilization of the poor and marginalized to make use of the new opportunities. This process is not free from obstacles and barriers.[12] Because the new dispensation works for transfer of power from the dominant to the marginalized, men to women and bureaucracy to elected representatives. People those who are in helm of affairs know that this Constitutional Amendment will not allow those who enjoyed power so far to be in power for ever. They know the full implications of the power transfer and as a result those who have been in power so far evolve new designs to keep power with them. "Elite Capture" has come in decentralization discourse because of this syndrome. Groups which are going to get advantage out of it have to make themselves aware of the new possibilities and opportunities that come through this new dispensation and organize themselves to take on the new opportunities. But the above task is through a process of struggle. The struggle is also a long drawn struggle and for which poor are to be prepared and facilitated. Who will facilitate the poor and who will be the part of the struggle of the marginalized groups to make use of this opportunity is the question. In this regard, academics have to play a crucial role from awareness creation and conscientisation to extending handhold support to the poor women, and other marginalized groups elected to the local governments. Theoretically speaking, middle class has a role in the transformative process of the society. Amending the Constitution is only a necessary condition for the establishment of a permanent local governance institutional arrangement at the grassroots.[13] But it is not a sufficient condition. Sufficient conditions are many. They are being given in the following Fig. 3.1 schematically.

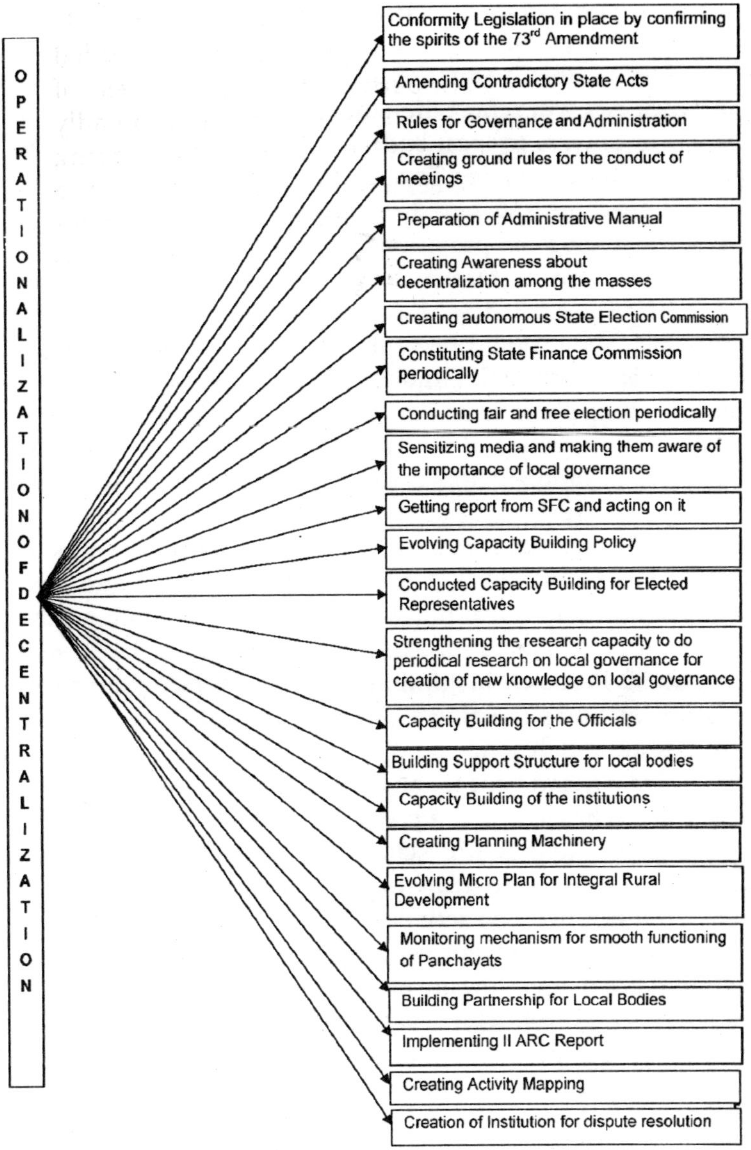

Fig. 3.1: Matrix on Oprationalization of Decentralization

First a confirmative legislation has to be passed in the Provincial Legislature by confirming the spirit of the 73rd Amendment to the Constitution of India. The State Government's Panchayat Act will reflect the will of the State Government in devolving powers to local bodies and in responding faith in peoples will and capacity. To operationalize the Act effectively, the State Governments have to remove or amend the State Acts which are having the provisions against the spirit of the 73rd Amendment and conformity legislation. Proper rules and by-laws have to be created and they are to be in place and are to be simplified. They should be in the form of a manual. It is the administrative manual. Simultaneously, awareness has to be created among the stakeholders about the new opportunities. It is a kind of marketing of the products of a company. It should be done as a company does marketing of its product. It should be done in a mission mode by adopting a market approach. Media, judiciary, academia, civil society and opinion-makers have to be conscientized and sensitized about the new dispensation and its implications.[14] In one judgement, the Supreme Court of India equated the power of Gram Sabha with Lok Sabha. Research institutions have to oversee the proper creation of State Election Commission and State Finance Commission and their functions from the perspective of the spirit of the 73rd Amendment to the Constitution of India. The State Government has to evolve a policy for capacity-building and to create a new leadership school to transform the elected representatives into transformational leaders to bring transformation in the society. Because there is no training policy for training the elected representatives and the available training institutions barring a few are not in shape with capacity to train leaders. A support structure has to be created to extend handhold support to the local bodies to deliver services and discharge their responsibilities. The whole range of activities have to be done by various agencies and of them State's role is pivotal.

By keeping the above Matrix of operationalization of decentralization of powers, a state has been evaluated as to what extent steps had been taken to implement the 73rd Amendment to the Constitution of India. This evaluation requires not a mechanical process. It needs an organic intellectual analysis. It is not a verification process. It is an in-depth analysis. Scholarly exercise can alone bring the reality. The following Table 3.1 will give how a state has taken efforts to decentralize powers to grassroots institution.

Table 3.1: Operationalization of Decentralization and Democratization in Tamil Nadu

Sl. No.	*Items*	*State*		
		Yes	*No*	*Partially*
1.	Conformity Legislation	√		
2.	Amending Contradictory State Acts		√	
3.	Rules for Governance and Administration			√
4.	Preparation of Administrative Manual		√	
5.	Awareness about Decentralization			√
6.	Creation of autonomous State Election Commission			√
7.	Conducting free and fair elections periodically			√
8.	Sensitizing media and making them aware of the importance of local governance			√
9.	Strengthening the capacity to do periodical research on local governance for creation of new knowledge on local governance			√
10.	Commissioning State Finance Commission periodically	√		
11.	Getting report from the State Finance Commission and acting on them			√
12.	Evolving Capacity-Building Policy		√	
13.	Conducted Capacity-Building for Elected Representatives			√
14.	Capacity-Building of the Officials			√
15.	Evolving micro-plan for integrated development		√	
16.	Monitoring mechanism for smooth functioning of Panchayats	√		
17.	Building support structure			√
18.	Building partnership		√	
19.	Implementing II ARC Report		√	
20.	Implementing Mani Shankar Aiyar Report			√
21.	Creating Activity Mapping		√	

Source: Computed from the works of the Rajiv Gandhi Chair for Panchayati Raj Studies, Gandhigram Rural Institute–Deemed University, Gandhigram.

Democratization

First time in Indian democracy a constitutionally created democratic governance structure is at the community level through the 73rd Amendment to the Constitution of India. Till then rural communities have been in the habit of following the community practices to regulate the affairs of the communities. One cannot expect the whole community will change itself from following the archaic community practices to the provisions of the Constitution. It is an obvious fact that Indian society is feudal in character and following the hierarchical caste system with economic inequalities which ultimately reflect in the attitude and behaviour of the people. Against such socio-economic background the new governance mechanism has to work at the grassroots. There is yet another force, the bureaucracy which all along established its hegemony over the community down below the district level has now to work under the elected representatives. The bureaucracy is not free from the influence of the social system. Thus, an array of forces at the community level are working against the practices of democracy and in this context the new governance mechanism has to deliberate, decide and allocate resources for development activities. In the rural areas, those who have been in the helm of affairs in the community system have to give space for the newly created Constitutional bodies for governance. This process will face lot of resistance covertly and overtly.

Before coming to the main argument of implementing the new dispensation, it is an imperative to dispel the cloud surrounded the concept—decentralization of powers. Because there are two kinds of operational definitions have been given to the concept "decentralization of powers". One is broader and encompassing assigned and assumed roles and responsibilities by using law of subsidiarity. Yet, another is narrower view of looking at decentralization of powers by treating the local bodies as institutions for implementing the schemes of the State and Central Governments. A narrower definition of decentralization of powers limits the potentials of the new local government. It has come for mere provisions of services alone. In reality, it has come for larger purposes. It has come for achieving economic development and social justice. The above objectives have to be achieved through a new process. It is through a participatory process. In the participatory process, the affected, weak and the marginalized have to be involved as participants. To enable them to participate in the process of development, they are to be empowered. Arrays of steps have to be taken to prepare the poor, women and other marginalized groups to participate in the process of governance and development. Further, it has to be done with a perspective. The perspective is that the development of the marginalized is not based on charity, but based on rights. Thus rights perspective should be kept in the backdrop of the governance at the grassroots. Thus, broader conceptualization of decentralization is the need of the hour. It has to be given by the opinion-makers and intellectuals who shape the public opinion. Otherwise, the bureaucracy will take the narrower and legal view of 'decentralization' which will not enable the people to release the energy.

Power transfer will not happen without a struggle and it is a time consuming process. It requires not only the political support. It needs the broader support of the intellectuals, media and the masses. This struggle has to be waged through non-violent means as advocated by M.K. Gandhi for achieving *Swaraj*. In the process of power transfer, people who assume responsibility and leadership in the local bodies have to discharge functions not only the assigned, but also assumed. It requires a new kind of leadership. It is not conventional managerial leadership, but it should be transformational leadership. It is creative, vibrant, visionary, revolutionary leadership. Attitude, behaviour, and activities of the leadership should enable the people to repose faith and confidence in him or her. Thus, this type of leadership has to be shaped. Electing a leader is in the hands of the people, but shaping the leadership is in the hands of the leadership schools. Hence, transformational leadership training has to be organized to enhance the capacity of the elected representatives of the people. It cannot be performed by the conventional state institute of rural development. It requires a new kind of institutions. It should be run not by the bureaucrats, but it should be run by the intellectuals and visionary leaders. It requires training module, exemplary intellectuals and leaders as trainers and training ambience. It can be done only by the institutions of higher order with creative individuals.

A very important organ of democracy promotion is media. In the last five to six decades media had been oriented to look at issues from the perspective of federal and regional governments and politics. But, now the paradigm of governance and development has been changed from "Top down" to "Bottom up". This new perspective needs understanding from media as they play a vital role in sharing and shaping opinion, perception and views of the public. Who will do this job is the major question. Media has to be sensitized and conscientized by the intellectuals of the higher learning institutions. Enormous preparation is needed on the part of the academics and intellectuals in the higher learning institutions.

A sound policy and programme of a government basically depends on sound knowledge base and sound knowledge base depends on a sound database. Unless, we have sound knowledge base we cannot expect a proper policy from the governments. Policy advocacy is being done at the federal government and regional governments on several issues. In the same way, policy advocacy has to be done for grassroots governance also. Vastness of the country with regional variations requires state specific advocacies. To do the exercise from every state a policy advocacy group is needed. Continuously, research has to be carried out on all the issues and aspects of local governance and development. Very poor research output has been witnessed so far from the intellectuals of the higher learning institutions and research institutions on local governance and local development issues. Still 68 per cent of the people live in the rural areas. 58 per cent of the people rely on agriculture for their livelihood. To look at the issues of the people in the rural areas from the perspective of local governance we need more number of researchers from social science branch of the higher learning institutions. Till today we are not able to form collegium of scholars to do research on the issues of rural local governance.

Micro-level participatory planning is integral part of the new paradigm of local governance. It is the missing aspect in local governance which is also a violation of a provision of the Constitution. Now, it has been reinforced by the Fourteenth Finance Commission of India through its recommendation. Who will assist the Panchayats to evolve a plan for development in the absence of a regular machinery of planning? It has to be done by the higher learning institutions. In India, database is weak and data collection process is not in a sound footing. Especially, data on poverty and households are utterly weak. But, now a new opportunity comes in the form of creating governance and administrative institutions on a permanent basis at every Gram Panchayat. By using this opportunity, a scientific data base can be created at every administrative unit especially on households. This could be done by the academic institutions.

To make the rural local bodies more vibrant and efficient an array of steps are needed. For many of the activities, academic institutions especially higher learning institutions can play a proactive role.

Democracy Promotional Activities

From Gram Sabha to micro-level participatory planning all are mentioned only in the 73rd Amendment to the Constitution of India as concepts. They are to be operationalized in the broader context of decentralization and democratization. Creating mere democratic institutions will not bring a democratic culture in a society which has emerged in federal cultural moorings. Hence, all the institutions have to be enabled to transact their business through democratic processes and procedures.[15] In the rural local governance process, we have Gram Sabha, Committees in Village Panchayats, Village Panchayat Council, Block Panchayat Council, Committees in Block Panchayat, District Ward Council, District Panchayat

Committees and District Planning Committees. All these institutions have to take decisions, allocate resources, spend the amount, execute the decisions and evaluate their activities and their impacts. To perform all those activities well laid procedures have to be evolved. These procedures have to reflect the core values of democracy. These procedures should reflect equality, respecting dissent voice, fairness and justice. From seating arrangement to allotting time to express their views in the meetings of all the institutions, procedures have to be evolved and they are to be followed not as ritual, but in letter and spirit. This process will bring disturbance to many in the rural areas. Ruling, dominance, suppression, oppression, obedience were the practices which are against equality.

Take the case of Gram Sabha. Gram Sabha is the parliament of the people at the grassroots. People should be oriented to participate in the Gram Sabha meeting. For enabling the people basics have to be evolved. Gram Sabha has certain mandatory functions and apart from the mandatory functions, it has to assume some responsibilities to develop a culture of democracy. Gram Sabha can be made as a discourse centre, a debating centre, a deliberation centre and a centre for dissemination of vital information on governance and development. Leading the members of Gram Sabha towards discourse require leadership. Effective, interesting and meaningful discourse in Gram Sabha depends on leadership. In such a way leadership has to be shaped. An informed and nurtured leader can alone lead a matured and informed debate in Gram Sabha. In Indian context, maintaining equality and dignity in the discourse of the forum is a difficult task. Like Gram Sabha, Panchayat Council meetings, Panchayat Committee meetings have to be conducted. In the same way at Panchayat level meetings have to be conducted. In Indian context, meetings have been made more of a rituals rather than evolving a meaningful decision-making process after a thorough discourse and deliberation. This could be possible only through evolving a manual (guidebook) for conduct of meetings. It should be just May's Parliamentary Practice Book. It should be a guidebook. It has to be prepared only by intellectuals.

Rules for the Conduct of the Meeting
(Gram Sabha, Committees of Panchayats, Panchayat Council)

- Ground Rules for Seating
- Ground Rules for Timing
- Ground Rules for Listening
- Ground Rules for Arguments
- Ground Rules for Language
- Ground Rules for Responses
- Ground Rules for Attire

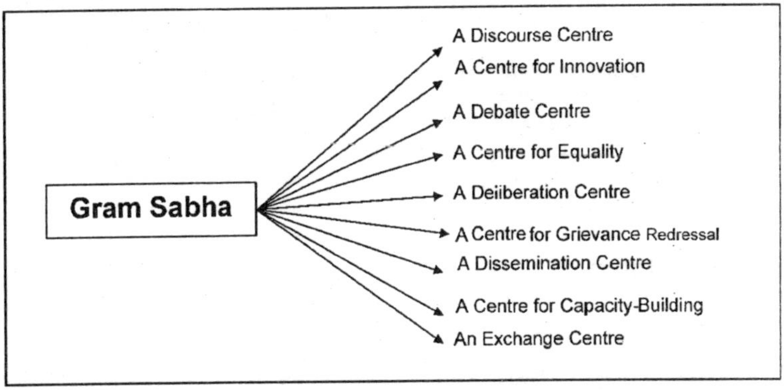

Box 3.1: What I gained through Gram Sabha?

A Gram Sabha Member (Ms. Mariamma, 62 years old) in Karisalpatti Gram panchayat in Dindigul District made an observation when our students are in the fieldwork. It is being reproduced here:

"Many of the government schemes are implemented by various departments and agencies in our village. Who is in which office, implemented the schemes of the government are not known to us, I have used Gram Sabha to track information. I got all the information only from the Gram Sabha. This is possible because the observer coming from Government Department to Gram Sabha and explain to us. My close relative has not received old age pension for several months and she was not able to move out from her house. When it was raised in the Gram Sabha the Gram Panchayat President took responsibility to get details from the concerned office. Promptly the President took step to help the old women. As a result, she got the pension. I am a wage earner in MGNREGA, and I was not sure of getting wages in time. Hence, I raised in the Gram Sabha meeting. I got reply. I am an unskilled labourer working in a farm. Panchayat operates drinking water supply when I am in the farm. I raised it in the Gram Sabha. Since, many of the women belong to my street raised the same—the timing of drinking water supply, it has been changed to suit our requirement. To me it is a parliament. I got this information from our SHG meeting."

Box 3.2: What I gained through Gram Sabha?

Mr. Muniasamy, a Gram Sabha member in Alamarathupatti Gram Panchayat in Dindigul District made an observation when our students went for a fieldwork. It is being reproduced here:

"Gram Sabha is a best place to demonstrate equality in an unequal society. Caste hierarchy is the reality in the rural areas. Untouchability is yet another reality operates in different forms in the villages. *Gram Sabha* is an instrument to change the mindset of the people. A *dalit* cannot sit along with the higher caste persons in any social function in the village settings. But in *Gram Sabha* I find that equality at least in sitting along with them. I regularly attend the Gram Sabha meeting only to enjoy that equality in the village by sitting with higher caste men and women. Everybody has to sit only on the floor. Further, I can ask questions in the Gram Sabha. Questioning a higher caste person in a village in unacceptable. But in Gram Sabha being a president he or she has to respond to the questions of all. I raise many questions and I get answers to my questions. I enjoy questioning. I enjoy sitting with a higher caste person. It gives joy and happiness. Being a *dalit* I can only realize the joy."

Here is a Model

Despite the promises of decentralization and performance of the rural local bodies in India, why political class and bureaucracy are not evincing interest in strengthening local bodies? is a major question daunting in the minds of exponents of democracy and decentralization. There are many reasons and of them one is the failure of the middle class and intellectuals in performing their catalytic role. In this context, I would like to dilate upon the activities of the Rajiv Gandhi Chair for Panchayati Raj Studies on strengthening Panchayati Raj in the last fifteen years. It is an account of voluntary activities evolved by a set of teachers in a small university by creating a chair in a Department. Rajiv Gandhi Chair for Panchayati Raj Studies in the Department of Political Science and Development Administration, Gandhigram Rural Institute—Deemed University has been created only by the teachers in the Department. It was the first Rajiv Gandhi Chair in India. It was not given by the UGC. By seeing the voluntary works of the teachers many donor agencies have funded the activities of the Chair. By seeing the activities of the Chair, a few Members of Parliament have contributed Rs. 40,000 lakhs to construct a building for the Chair. In the whole of India Rajiv

Gandhi Chair of Gandhigram Rural Institute has got a separate building. It carried out wide range of activities to strengthen

Table 3.2: Activities of the Rajiv Gandhi Chair for Panchayati Raj Studies

Sl. No.	*Activities*	*Support*	*Coverage*
1.	To create awareness among the people about New Panchayati Raj System.	Formed a network called Tamil Nadu Campaign for Panchayati Raj (TCPR).	The whole state. It conducted an extensive work.
2.	To exert pressure on the government to conduct the election.	Submitted petitions to Governor. Worked for inclusion of panchayat election in the election manifesto of the DMK and TMC during 1996.	
3.	To conduct voter awareness programme	With the support of PRIA and the Hunger Project pre-election vote awareness programme was conducted by the Chair with the support large number of civil society organizations.	The whole state has been covered.
4.	To conduct the training programme for elected representatives	Prepared training module with the support of CAPART and Rajiv Gandhi Foundation.	For the whole state.
5.	To conduct the training programme for Elected Women Representatives	Prepared training module with the support of the Hunger Project.	For Tamil Nadu elected women representatives.
6.	To conduct training programme for the Dalit Elected Representatives	Prepared the training module with the support of PRIA.	For Tamil Nadu Dalit leaders.
7.	Leadership training	The chair conducted training programmes for 8000 Gram Panchayat Presidents. It was supported by CAPART, the Hunger Project and Government of Tamil Nadu.	For the entire state.
8.	To assist the administration	Administrative manual has been prepared and published both in English and Tamil.	For Tamil Nadu.
9.	To sensitise and conscientise the media	Media workshops have been conducted with the support of the Hunger Project.	Entire state.
10.	Establish handhold support for women leaders	Elected women representatives federation has been created and it was assisted by the Chair.	Entire state.
11.	Establish handhold support for *Dalit* leaders	Elected Dalit representatives federation has been created and it was assisted by the Chair.	Entire state.
12.	Establish handhold support for local body leaders	One local body supplement in a Newspaper was published for one year.	For the whole state.

Source: Rajiv Gandhi Chair, Ten Years of Activities on Decentralization of Powers, Gandhigram: Rajiv Gandhi Chair for Panchayati Raj Studies, 2014.

Panchayati Raj Institutions in Tamil Nadu. To give an account of the activities in nutshell, they are given in Table 3.2.

Conclusion

What aimed at India through the 73rd Amendment to the Constitution of India is to decentralize powers to local bodies through a process of democratization. Decentralization has to happen through democratic means and that is why, it is called democratic decentralization. Even the representative democratic institutions are struggling to keep the democratic values in the attitude and behaviour of the people who are involved in decision-making. One has to wonder how it will happen at the community level where all antithetical practices to democratic values are in operation. To make it happen a sufficient condition has to be created for democratization while decentralizing powers. Mere enactment of Act is only a necessary condition, but putting the necessary wherewithal will create a sufficient condition for effective decentralization. Hence, democratization is as important as decentralization. Both have potentials. Both play complementary to each other. Necessary conditions have been created by both Central Government and State Governments. Sufficient conditions have to be created by the civil society organizations, media, training institutions and the intellectuals. For democracy promotion ground rules creation and effective implementation could be done only by the higher learning institutions. Social Science Departments in higher learning institutions can do democracy promotional activities. To demonstrate how it could be done, I have explained the activities of the Rajiv Gandhi Chair for Panchayati Raj Studies of Gandhigram Rural Institute in the area of democratic decentralization of powers. It requires only passion not mandate from anybody.

NOTES

1. Myron Weiner, 1989, *Indian Paradoxes*, New Delhi: Sage Publication.

2. Rajendra Vora and Suhas Palshikar (eds.), 2004, *Indian Democracy: Meanings and Practices*, New Delhi: Sage Publication.
3. Peter Mair, 2008, "Democracies" in Daniel Caramani (ed.), *Comparative Politics*, New York: Oxford University Press.
4. Paul Ginsborg, 2009, *Democracy Crisis and Renewal*, London: Profile Books.
5. Jean Baechler, 1998, *Democracy: An Analytical Survey*, New Delhi: National Book Trust, India.
6. M.K. Gandhi, 1960, *Hind Swaraj*, Ahamedabad: Navjeevan Publications.
7. James Manor, 2010, Local Governance in Niraja Gopal Jayal and Pratap Bhanu Mehta (eds.), *The Oxford Companion to Politics in India*, New Delhi: Oxford University Press.
8. James Manor, 1999, *The Political Economy of Decentralization*, Washington DC: The World Bank Publication.
9. Rajani Kothari, 2005, *Rethinking Democracy*, New Delhi: Orient Longman.
10. Arend Lijphart, 1982, *Democracy in Plural Societies: A Comparative Explanation*, Bombay: Popular Prakashan.
11. Jayaprakash Narayan, Presidential Address in the Fourth National All India Panchayat Parishad Conference held in Bangalore on 18th July, 1964.
12. Barbara Geddes, 2007, "What Causes Democratization?" in Carles Boix and Susan C. Stokes (eds.), *The Oxford Hand Book of Comparative Politics*, New York: Oxford University Press.
13. Robert A. Dahl, *Authority in a Good Society*, New Delhi: Allied Publishers Pvt. Ltd.
14. Peter Burnell, 2008, "Promoting Democracy" in Daniel Caramani (ed.), *Comparative Politicism*, New York: Oxford University Press.
15. Jacques Thomassen, 2009, "Democratic Values", Russel J. Dalton and Hans-Dieter Klingemann (eds.), *The Oxford Hand Book of Political Behaviour*, New York: Oxford University Press.

4

Democracy Promotion through Decentralization of Powers in India

Introduction

'Decentralization' is a new governance mechanism initiated not only in India, but also in more than sixty countries in the world through different ways from amending the Constitution of the country to passing an executive order to create an institution of governance at the grassroots.[1] It has been initiated along with democracy promotion, economic globalization and dynamic developmentalism through communication revolution. Thirty years have gone and many changes have been witnessed both positive and negative due to the impact of decentralization, globalization, democratization and developmentalism. Many of the implications have been investigated. Perspective approach and framework vary from discipline to discipline while analyzing the implications of decentralization. Economists have contributed substantially with an objective of influencing policies of the Governments. Attempts have been made globally, nationally, regionally and locally to assess to what extent globalization, decentralization democratization and developmentalism have been operationalized by the Governments and to what extent they have created the intended impact in the society.[2] Each one becomes a movement in the world and its implementation varies from region to region depending on the socio-political conditions of the society.

Among the major aspects, decentralization draws the attention of the bilateral and multilateral development agencies as it raises hope to address many of the development issues which have not been effectively addressed by the federal and regional governments not only in India, but also in many of the countries in the world. Potentials of decentralization prompt the development agencies to incentivize the federal and State Governments to promote decentralization in the developing countries.[3] It is to be noted here that the decentralization initiated at present is different from that of the past. The present dispensation of decentralization is part of globalization and to facilitate globalization. It is one of the arguments. There is yet another argument that decentralization is part of globalization. No doubt, it is a mechanism by which positive outcome of globalization can be harnessed and negative could be either avoided or to be tackled through decentralization.

In India, at present, democratic decentralization has come through a process of constitutionalization. It has raised hope among different stakeholders that it would deepen democracy, achieve economic development and social justice at the grassroots and, ultimately, it would result in empowering the people mostly the poor through their participation in governance and development.[4] From World Bank to UN agencies, all development agencies have evinced keen interest in decentralization process in India. India is not a small country. The total number of representatives involved in decision-making process and in governance is in the order of three millions. It surpasses the total population of some of the developed countries. If this number of representatives are totally engaged in governance, the expected change and transformation would be huge. With this expectation the donor agencies have evinced keen interest in decentralization in India. Twenty years have gone and real question comes from every quarter whether the process of decentralization was effective and has it created expected impact in governance, society and the lives of the people at the grassroots and if not why?[5] It is raised in the context of changing regime at the Centre taking position and accepting the recommendations of the Fourteenth Finance Commission. By accepting Fourteenth Finance Commission recommendations by the Central Government it gives a new direction for the state and local Governments that they are not mere implementing agencies to spend money. In a true spirit of cooperative federalism, the State and local governments have to take major responsibilities to address the critical issues of development. Further, it is asked to what extent the devolved powers have created transformation at the community level. As a sequence what needs to be done to strengthen the process of decentralization has to be discussed. Finally, where are we now in decentralization in India? These are the major questions to be investigated in this exercise.

Methodology

To find answer to the above questions, the available research reports prepared by Government of India, documents prepared by bilateral and multilateral agencies and research studies conducted by donor agencies have been consulted apart from the research reports prepared by individual scholars in the traditional academic institutions and research companies and agencies. It is a well known fact that scholars from the US and the other western countries have done extensive pan-India studies and brought out results. Equally, Government of India and some research organizations brought out series of reports. All the reports and documents have been consulted. It is to be noted that pan-India studies are limited and state specific studies are more in number. More number of studies concentrated on devolution process. Only a few studies concentrated on the impact of devolution in the functioning of the institutions and its implications in the life of the people at the community level. For the assessment and evaluation of devolution and its implications pan-India studies are taken into account. State specific studies have also been consulted and taken into account in our perusal and analysis.

Emerging Trends

Democratic decentralization as a major governance reform initiative undertaken by the Government of India for a larger purpose at grassroots in India. It is the result of a major reform initiative taken up in the world in the beginning of 1970s as many of the countries in the world witnessed the failures of the centralized governance mechanism introduced after the Second World War.[6] Faith and belief in centralized governance machinery have gone down based on the poor performance of the big governments in the world. When the leaders of the countries were on search of alternative mechanism to the existing governing arrangements decentralization came handy to handle many of the problems of the people at the community level by involving the people who are affected. Thus, it gained prominence and acceptance from all sections of the society barring those who are in power both in the Central and State Governments. At that point of time the concept gained currency in India. It came along with globalization of economy. Democratic decentralization process is fairly a complex story in India.[7] It has got many promises.

To fulfil the promises of decentralization sufficient enabling conditions have to be created at the ground. Performance level varies from region to region, country to country and province to province depending on the enabling conditions created for decentralization. Further, one has to understand that it has got limitations also. In Indian context, despite limitations, the decentralized governance institutions have delivered services effectively and efficiently.[8] Despite an array of barriers in the process of decentralization, it delivered successfully goods and services to the people. It sounds that if all the barriers are removed and sufficient conditions are created, its delivery will be much more than what it has delivered so far. Having seen the worthiness and achievements of these institutions, why political and policy communities are not taking earnest interest to push this institution further, is the major question raised by the researchers. It is to be remembered here that after India got

Independence Nehru wanted to create a Panchayati Raj. He created a Ministry and appointed S.K. Dey as Minister for Community Development, Panchayati Raj and Cooperatives. He has developed a framework of Panchayati Raj.[9] But that attempt also met with failures. While delivering the presidential address in All India Panchayat Parishad in 1964, Jayaprakash Narayan after the demise of Nehru captured all the causes for its failure.[10] He said that decentralization will enable the poor and marginalized to move closer to power but that is not being liked by many who are in power. Decentralization of power can be achieved only through a process of building a mass movement in India otherwise power to the people is a pipe dream. India is known for many rhetoric and of them decentralization of power to the people is also one. It is a phenomenon in India that a force invisibly is working towards keeping the poor and marginalized away from Government. Hence, one could see a perceptible gap between the mass and the Government of India.

The same policy communities silently work for globalization despite opposition among the masses. Whereas they did not work for decentralization effectively and efficiently even though it has got the support of the masses. To enable the masses to make use of decentralization, State Governments have to take an array of steps sequentially, systematically and organically. They are given in the form of a diagram in Fig. 4.1.

If we check with the above parameters one can see where the local governments stand in India. Below given table 4.1 reflects the status of devolution of powers in a State.

Ministry of Panchayati Raj, Government of India has taken earnest efforts to evaluate annually the devolution process of the States and incentivizing the states according to their level of devolution of powers. This has not created any impact in the devolution process of the States. People who are in the State Government are evincing keen interest in transforming power down below to them. Essentially, they look at the same as a ploy to weaken the state by centralizing powers from the State and decentralizing powers to local bodies from the State. The

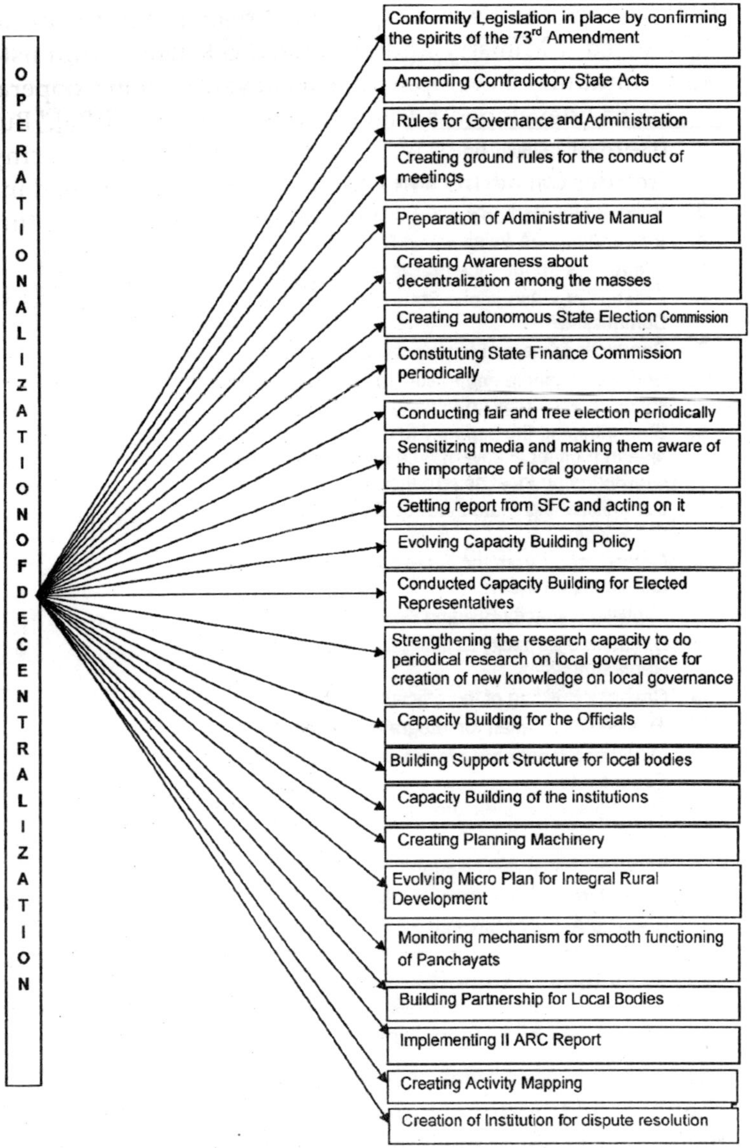

Fig. 4.1: Matrix on Operationalization of Decentralization

Table 4.1: Reflect the status of devolution of Power in a State.

Sl. No.	*Items*	*State*		
		Yes	*No*	*Partially*
1.	Conformity Legislation	√		
2.	Amending Contradictory State Acts		√	
3.	Rules for Governance and Administration			√
4.	Preparation of Administrative Manual		√	
5.	Awareness about decentralization			√
6.	Creation of autonomous State Election Commission			√
7.	Conducting free and fair elections periodically			√
8.	Sensitizing media and making them aware of the importance of local governance			√
9.	Strengthening the capacity to do periodical research on local governance for creation of new knowledge on local governance			√
10.	Commissioning State Finance Commission periodically	√		
11.	Getting report from the State Finance Commission and acting on them			√
12.	Evolving Capacity Building Policy		√	
13.	Conducted Capacity Building for Elected Representatives			√
14.	Capacity Building of the officials			√
15.	Evolving micro-plan for integrated development		√	
16.	Monitoring mechanism for smooth functioning of Panchayats	√		
17.	Building support structure			√
18.	Building partnership		√	
19.	Implementing II ARC Report		√	
20.	Implementing Mani Shankar Aiyar Report			√
21.	Creating Activity Mapping		√	

Source: Computed from the works of the Rajiv Gandhi Chair for Panchayati Raj Studies, Gandhigram Rural Institute—Deemed University, Gandhigram.

reality is however weak it is, it exists and functions. It brings changes and transformations. To assess the impact of the local bodies in the life of the households in rural areas yet another simple framework has been developed.

By using this framework what difference the local institutions have made has been assessed. Many micro-studies

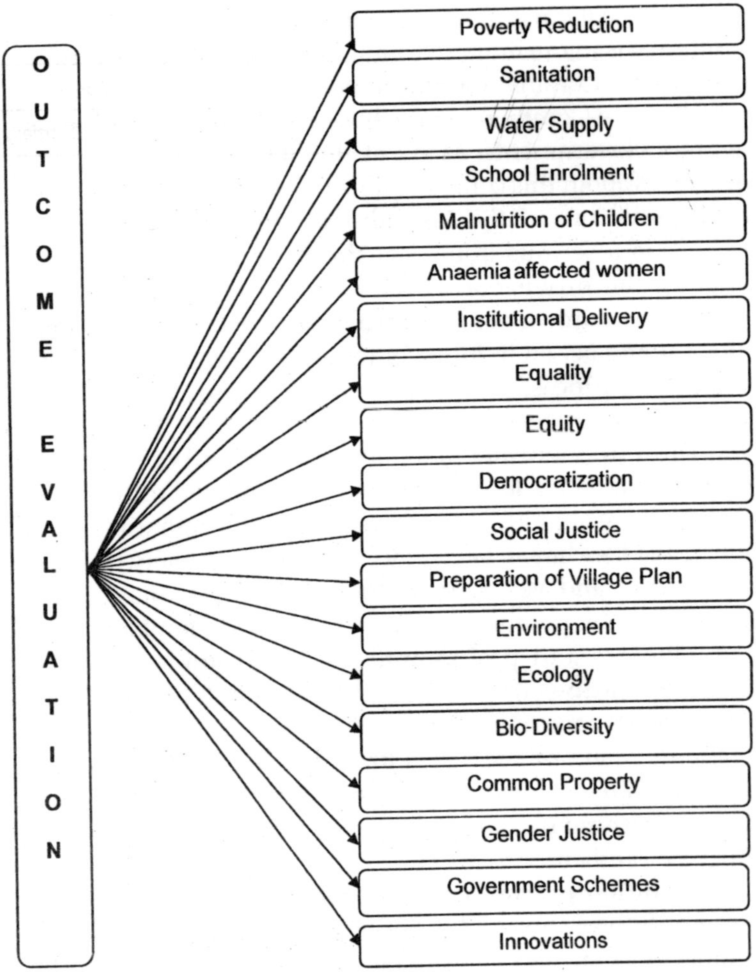

have been conducted. Significant transformations have been achieved.[11]

It is no doubt that corruption has been reduced in the development sector considerably after the establishment of decentralized governance mechanism at the ground. Yet the number of people involved in corruption has been increased.[12] Many of the core principles of the 73rd and 74th Amendments to the Constitution of India have not been put into practice. The State Governments barring a few are reluctant to give powers to local governments.[13] Constituting District Planning Committee is a core initiative but it is not created. Constituting State Finance Commission and acting on the recommendations of the Finance Commission are the essential responsibilities of the State Governments. Many of the State Governments are not serious about this core functions.[14] They are really violation of the provisions of the Amendment to the Constitution of India. It is a serious issue that the State Governments are violating the provisions of the Constitutions. Neither, the Central Government nor the judiciary nor the civil society take note of it and act on it. In many fora it has been raised. There should be a process by which devolution process has to be pushed and proceeded. It was believed that the Central Government would act sympathetically towards decentralization as decentralization was initiated only by the Central Government. It appears to be sympathetic as the Ministry of Panchayati Raj has been acting proactively towards panchayats[15] and yet many of the Ministries of the Central Government by passing the Panchayats while implementing their schemes and programmes at the ground. From the research studies it is inferred that most of the State Governments have refused to devolve funds, functionaries and functions. Many of the states first shown some enthusiasm latter they are reluctant to pay such attention. Many of the State Governments have taken away some of the powers conferred on them.

Devolution process has been made much complicated. Representatives those who are in power at grassroots face plethora of problems in governance and administration.[16] Their capacity has to be enhanced through a process of capacity-building. But it does not take place effectively and professionally. Training infrastructure has been developed, but quality training is the problem. Poor and marginalized groups tend to gain advantage through decentralization. Despite some progress in delivery of service and deepening of democracy, the States are not willing to part power with local governments. A slowdown has surfaced in decentralization process. As a result, many donor agencies have moved away from decentralization activities. A large number of scholars who have evinced keen interest in decentralization research have opted out from continuing the research in decentralization. Many civil society organizations who have involved massively in decentralization have withdrawn from these works and moved over to other areas as they found enormous resources. Yet local governance institutions exist and they continue to function.

Time and again it is stressed that at the Panchayat level data base is not maintained and as a result there is no proper accounting mechanism established. As a result, there is no consolidation of data base for income and expenditure which resulted in poor policy advocacy from the perspective of panchayats. For the past twenty years State Finance Commissions found it very difficult to make scientific and precise recommendation for resource management at Panchayat level. Everyone knows that lowest unit of governance is the appropriate mechanism to keep household data, but nobody bothers to develop a discourse on this issue.

Although the decentralization exercises have been looked into from the perspective of the 73rd and 74th Amendments to the Constitution of India and not from the perspective of the states.[17] Panchayati Raj System is a State subject which has to be looked at from the perspective of States as it warrants in the context of cooperative federalism. Realistically speaking decentralization has to be implemented only by the State Governments. Justice Venkatachalaiya report has recommended certain Constitutional reforms pertinent to the 73rd and 74th Amendments to the Constitution of India.[18] Later the Centre-State Relations Committee has made certain recommendations on the same subjects.[19] Yet nothing came out from the Government. Following the above, Second Administrative Reform Commission has made more realistic actionable recommendations based on the performance of the institutions.[20] It is a pity that none of the Secretaries from the Government of India had put a road map to implement the recommendations of the Commission in their respective Ministries. When the Central Government is not able to consider its own recommendations how one can expect the

State Governments to implement the recommendation of the Committee reports.

The very character of democracy has been changed because of the creation of Gram Sabha for participation of citizens in the process of governance and development has not been activated by creating ground rules for the conduct of Gram Sabha. Rules for participation, structure for participation have to be created for enabling the poor to participate in Gram Sabha meeting. The deliberative aspect of this democracy is missed. To get the full potentials of Gram Sabha enough ground rules and enabling conditions have to be created. These steps have to be taken by the State Governments. Adequate steps had not been taken by the State Governments in this regard.[21]

Box 4.1: What I gained through Gram Sabha?

A Gram Sabha Member (Ms. Mariamma, 62 Years old) in Karisalpatti Gram Panchayat in Dindigul District made an observation when our students are in the fieldwork. It is being reproduced here:

"Many of the Government schemes are implemented by various departments and agencies in our village. Who is in which office, implemented the schemes of the Government are not known to us, I have used Gram Sabha to track information. I got all the information only from the Gram Sabha. This is possible because the observer coming from Government Department to Gram Sabha and explain to us. My close relative has not received old age pension for several months and she was not able to move out from her house. When it was raised in the Gram Sabha, the Gram Panchayat President took responsibility to get details from the concerned office. Promptly the President took step to help the old women. As a result, she got the pension. I am a wage earner in MGNREGA, and I was not sure of getting wages in time. Hence, I raised in the Gram Sabha meeting. I got reply. I am an unskilled labourer working in a farm. Panchayat operates drinking water supply. When I am in the farm panchayat operates water supply. I could not fetch water from the public tape as I was in the farm. I raised it in the Gram Sabha. Since, many of the women belong to my street raised the same the timing of drinking water supply, it has been changed to suit our requirement. To me it is a parliament. I got this information from our SHG meeting."

Governance and administration is always complex in nature in India and it needs to be simplified to enable the citizens to participate in the process of governance and administration as stakeholders. Based on the Act, simplified rules have to be issued by the State Governments and they are

Box 4.2: What I gained through Gram Sabha?

Mr. Muniasamy, a Gram Sabha member in Alamarathupatti Gram Panchayat in Dindigul District made an observation when our students went for a fieldwork. It is being reproduced here:

"Gram Sabha is a best place to demonstrate equality in an unequal society. Caste hierarchy is the reality in the rural areas. Untouchability is yet another reality operates in different forms in the villages. Gram Sabha is an instrument to change the mindset of the people. A *dalit* cannot sit along with the higher caste persons in any social function in the village settings. But in Gram Sabha I find that equality at least in sitting along with them. I regularly attend the Gram Sabha meeting only to enjoy that equality in the village by sitting with higher caste men and women. Everybody has to sit only on the floor. Further, I can ask questions in the Gram Sabha. Questioning a higher caste person in a village in unacceptable. But, in Gram Sabha being a president he or she has to respond to the questions of all. I raise many questions and I get answers to my questions. I enjoy questioning. I enjoy sitting with a higher caste person. It gives joy and happiness. Being a dalit I can only realize the joy."

to be compiled. They should be in the form of administrative manual and it is to be given to every Gram Panchayats, every Block Panchayats and every District Panchayats. It is not taking place seriously and as a result governance becomes secretive which threatens the elected representatives of the local bodies. Rules for governance and administration should be made open to public social audit could be possible only when the people are of the procedures and process of administration and implementation of schemes and programmes. Up to Gram Sabha members it should reach. Has it reached them? is a big question and for which there is no answer. Then only one can follow the accountability. Barring a few states there is no administrative manual for panchayat administration.[22] Absence of administrative manual will pave the way for corruption and domination of officials over the elected representatives. In the same way the elected representatives have to be trained in governance and administration on a sustainable basis. But in India so far there is no training structure. We have only training institutions with facility but delivery is poor as the trainers are drawn from Government Departments as they are unwanted in Government Departments. In India, there is no training culture for elected representatives whether they are Members of Parliament or Members of Legislative Assembly.

But there is a system and process of training for local body representatives. Twenty years have gone, we have three million representatives have to be involved in governing process. But there is no comprehensive capacity-building exercise to be carried out throughout the period on a sustainable basis. There is no training policy to build the capacity of the elected representatives in India. Yet, another issue has been probed locally and all over India whether the elected women representatives have performed well and if not why.?[23] It is demonstrated unequivocally that there is a significant impact of reservation of seats for women in local governance on the process of governance and development at the grassroots. Despite several barriers and limitations, they exhibit their performance.[24]

In this context, the Fourteenth Finance Commission had made a set of recommendations to alter the paradigm of governance at grassroots. By this recommendation it empowers Gram Panchayats to evolve a development plan for five years and make use of the united funds flow from the Central Government to Gram Panchayats while preparing the plan, all the Government Departments, schemes have to be synergistically integrated.[25] Every Gram Panchayat has to prepare a plan. But there is no planning machinery at the ground. It is to be done only with the help of either academic and research institutions or the civil society organizations. Now, there are guidelines for preparing model panchayats and in the same way there are guidelines for academic institutions to work with communities through a new scheme called Unnata Bharata Abhiyan. They are to be utilized effectively to conduct this planning exercise at the grassroots.[26]

There is a debate on the meaning of decentralization. The concept of decentralization is not being explained properly in India. Decentralization is a process of transferring powers from highest decision-making institution to the lowest decision-making unit nearest to the community-based on the principle of subsidiarity. But in India, it is defined as a process of transfer of power from the State Government to the lowest unit of decision-making at the community level in the context of centralization in the name of globalization. Decentralization has been looked at from different perspectives based on the disciplines and many of the policy advocacies are made by the economists as they did substantial pan-India studies with the support of many donor agencies. Regional and local studies have been conducted by sociologists and political scientists and did policy advocacy at the regional level. Old theorist on local governance has been challenged by the new evidences arising out of pan-India studies. Yet, theoretical conjectures are not evolved till date even though there are enough scope for it.

Time and again economists who have gone through the reports of State Finance Commissions and Central Finance Commission have indicated the major problem in Panchayat administration. The absence of database for income and expenditure of the local bodies indicate the non-seriousness on the part of the State officials which ultimately keep the policy-makers not to evolve scientific policies for effective management of local bodies. In the last twenty years we could not see a perspective comprehensive policy note from any organization based on pan-India research studies.

In the last thirty years world has witnessed the surge of research institutions to do research on the issues of market and for which research grants are sanctioned in millions. But for research in decentralization and its implication very limited institutional arrangements have been created and a small position of public funds are made available for carry out research activities in the area of decentralization. Pan-India studies show the positive implications of decentralization, but at the same time the decentralization process is not smooth to produce the same results continuously. Hence, it is necessary to take concrete steps to strengthen local bodies. Reservation of women has significant impact on empowerment of poor and the marginalized. In terms of service provision local bodies have demonstrated its abilities. Service delivery is yet another important area where local bodies are making their mark. It is worthwhile to consider for policy advocacy. In India studies show that per capita bribery is higher than per capita tax. It is a major finding but it has to be examined further as to how corruption could be reduced and tax base could be increased for local bodies. From the world studies, it has been informed that many of the State Governments are not willing to take hard decisions to bring an alternative paradigm of governance from the perspective of resource management.

What is the Need?

Even after twenty years of the new experiment there is no platform for proper policy advocacy for decentralization and democratization and development at grassroots. Research conducted so far on decentralization, development at grassroots and democratization of the communities is scanty, sporadic and region specific. Pan-Indian studies are rare. No worthwhile academy has been established in India to conduct studies on the above subjects. There is a National Academy in the name of National Institute of Rural Development and Panchayati Raj in Hyderabad meant for guiding the policy community in India. It is a national think tank. What is the contribution of the institute towards policy advocacy on this area? There is yet another institution—Institute of Rural Management, Anand. Huge public money has been spent for this institute by the Central Government for its policy work. What set of policies have come out from the institute. As stated by Jayaprakash Narayan in 1964, India needs a people's movement for power transfer. Despite the best efforts of Jawaharlal Nehru and S.K. Dey through their own party in power at the Centre and States decentralization could not be achieved as they desired. Decentralization could not see much progress as much obstacles and barriers were in the process of decentralization. That is why Jayaprakash Narayan wanted a people's movement for power transfer. Power transfer is not only from the State Government to local government, but also from Central Government to State Government as in the name of globalization more powers are centralized in the name of reform. Decentralization is being conceptualized now for pro- globalization. Decentralization has to be conceptualized to mobilize the poor and the marginalized to participate in the governance process at the grassroots and thereby globalization has to be made to work for poor through decentralization. Through their participation, the accountability system established so far in governance and administration has to be changed and thereby it should be oriented towards downward not upward. It is not financial accountability but performance accountability.

By mobilizing the masses for participation in governance at grassroots a new polity could be evolved and it will be a development politics and people's politics. To perform the above task, an academy has to be started and it has to work on the issues of decentralized governance, development, administration and their implications in the transformation of the rural communities and societies. A new training policy has to be evolved. It is for preparing transformational leaders to local bodies through capacity-building exercises. The existing training institutions have to be converted into new leadership schools. They should be kept out of State Government control. They should be autonomous. They can be attached with universities. In every State an administrative manual for local governance has to be prepared in the respective regional language that should be in people's language. That manual is a guiding book for local governance administration. This is very essential for ensuring accountability at panchayat level. In the absence of planning machinery at the ground, a detailed guideline can be prepared either by the State Government or Central Government as to how educational and research institutions can help the Panchayats to prepare development plan. For rural development policy-making and planning, reliable data base is an imperative need. Till date we could not present a reliable data set to policy-making body. It is the need of the hour. An interview schedule prepared for this available in NCAER and based software has to be prepared. It could be used for preparation of a strong scientific data set with the help of higher learning institution. A suitable mechanism has to be evolved to maintain and update the data set.

NOTES

1. Fumihiko Saito, 2011, "Decentralization" in Mark Bevir (ed.), *The Sage Handbook of Governance*, Washington DC: Sage Publications, pp. 484-500.
2. World Bank, 2008, *Decentralization in Client Countries: An Evaluation of World Bank Support 1990 to 2007*, Washington DC: World Bank.
3. James Manor, 1999, *The Political Economy of Democratic Decentralization*, Washington DC: World Bank.
4. Government of India, 2001, *Report of the Task Force on Panchayati Raj Institutions*, New Delhi: Government of India.
5. Mani Shankar Aiyar, 2013, *Towards Holistic Panchayati Raj: Twentieth Anniversary Report of the Expert Committee on Leveraging Panchayats for Efficient Delivery of Public Goods and Services*, Vols. I & II, New Delhi: Government of India.
6. James Manor, 2012, "Perspectives on Decentralization" in *The Imperative of Good Local Governance: Challenges of the Next Decade of Decentralization*, (eds.) Joakim Ojendal and Ankis Delinas, United States: United Nations University Press.
7. D.G. Gupta, 2004, *Decentralization: Need for Reform*, New Delhi: Concept Publishing Company.
8. Hari K. Nagarajan, Hans P. Binswanger Mkhize and S.S. Meenakshisundaram, 2015, *Decentralization and Empowerment for Rural Development*, New Delhi: Foundation Books.
9. Inaugural Address of Jawaharlal Nehru in Nagore, Rajasthan on 2nd October, 1959 while inaugurating the Panchayati Raj, *All India Congress Committee Economic Review 1960*, (The speech was in Hindi. It was translated into English).
10. Presidential Address of Jayaprakash Narayan in the Fourth National All India Panchayat Parishad Conference, Bangalore on 18th July, 1964. All India Panchayat Parishad, *Panchayati Raj: Perspective and Programme*, New Delhi: All India Panchayat Parishad, 1965.
11. G. Palanithurai, M.A. Thirunavukkarasu and G. Uma, 2007, *Change Makers at Grassroots Local Governance in Action*, New Delhi: Concept Publishing Company.
12. James Manor, 2010, "Local Governance" in Niraja Gopal Jayal and Pratap Bhanu Mehta (eds.), *The Oxford Companion to Politics in India*, New Delhi: Oxford University Press, pp. 61-79.
13. G. Mathew and N. Buch (eds.), 2011, *Status of Panchayati Raj in the States and Union Territories in India*, New Delhi: Concept Publishing Company (P) Ltd.
14. PRIA, 2001, *The State of Panchayats*, New Delhi: PRIA.
15. Government of India, 2010, *Compilation of Important Correspondence and Minutes of Major Meetings*, New Delhi: Ministry of Panchayati Raj.

16. Government of India, 2006, *The State of the Panchayats: A Mid-Term Review and Appraisal 2006*, New Delhi: Ministry of Panchayati Raj, 2006; Government of India, *Report of the Working Group on Democratic Decentralization and Panchayati Raj Institutions*, New Delhi: Planning Commission, Government of India.
17. Tata Institute of Social Sciences, 2015, *How Effective in Devolution across Indian States: Insights from the Field-Devolution Report 2014-15*, New Delhi: Ministry of Panchayati Raj, Government of India.
18. Government of India, 2002, *Report of National Commission to Review the Working of the Constitution*, Vols. I & II, New Delhi: Ministry of Law, Justice and Company Affairs.
19. Government of India, *Report of the Second Commission on Centre-State Relations*, Vols. I & II, New Delhi: Government of India.
20. Government of India, 2007, "Local Governance: An Inspiring Journey to the Future" Vol. II, *Second Administrative Reforms Commissions Report*", New Delhi: Government of India.
21. G. Palanithurai (ed.), 2015, *Deliberative Democracy*, New Delhi: MJP Publishers.
22. In Rajiv Gandhi Chair we took initiative to prepare manual for administration. G. Palanithurai, *Tamil Nadu Rural Local Bodies: Responsibilities and Process (Tamil) Manual for Local Body Leaders*, Chennai: Bharathi Puthakalayam, 2011; G. Palanithurai and *et al.*, 2006, *Handbook of Tamil Nadu Panchayat Administration*, New Delhi: Concept Publishing Company.
23. Government of India, 2008, *Study on Elected Women Representatives in Panchayati Raj Institutions*, New Delhi: Ministry of Panchayati Raj.
24. K. Deininger, H. Nagarajan and S. Paul "Can Political Reservations Empower Women and Affect Economic Outcomes? Evidence from Rural India", *NCAER working papers on Decentralization and Rural Governance in India*, No. 4, 2012; S. Kaushik, 1998, *Participation of Women in Panchayati Raj in India: A Stock Taking*, New Delhi: National Commission for Women.
25. Order No. 13 (32) FFC/FCD/2015-16, Government of India, Ministry of Finance, Department of Expenditure (Finance Commission Division) dated: 8th October, 2015. Guidelines for the implementations of recommendations of Fourteenth for Finance Commission (FC XIV) with regard to local bodies grant.
26. Order F. No. 19-8/2014 –TS.1 (Sectt), Government of India, Ministry of Human Resource Development, Department of Higher Education, Dated: 24th August, 2015 (Unnat Bharat Abhiyan).

5

Nehru's Framework of Panchayati Raj and Rural Development

Introduction

Even after sixty seven years of experience in democratic governance, India is still in minimal democracy.[1] Further, it is characterized as institutional democracy without having much practices of core values of democracy in Indian society and polity. Still, democratization process continues in political sphere[2], but in society, it is rare to observe. The need of the hour is social democracy.[3] It is a well known fact that the social conditions are not conducive for promotion of democratic values in Indian society. It is also an axiomatic truth that quality of democracy determine quality of governance and quality of service and goods provided by the Government to the people. Poor quality of democracy cannot deliver good governance. Poor democracy performs only minimum services that too with poor quality.[4] Despite the poor socio-economic conditions at the dawn of Independence the founding fathers of India nurtured and sown the seeds of democracy in Indian polity for governance with much hope and faith. Core values of democracy had been nurtured through representative democracy by electing representatives from Gram Panchayat to National Parliament through adult suffrage and enabled the institutions to function democratically. In the course of development and promotion of democracy, electoral process got strengthened[5], but disseminating the core values of democracy into the society gets stagnated or challenged by the social forces and as a result we find deficit in democracy.[6] To meet this deficit the new wave of decentralization had been initiated through a Constitutional process.[7] Even in the new context decentralization gets stagnated.[8] In this context, it is necessary to revisit the foundations laid by the founding fathers to democratize, the Indian society through rural local governance. Since, Jawaharlal Nehru took initiative and gave shape to Panchayati Raj in India after Independence, it is felt that it is necessary to analyse to what extent Jawaharlal Nehru solidly laid the foundation for democratization of Indian society and why it was stagnated in the midway is to be investigated and explained. No doubt, it is a new narrative for democracy promotion through institutional governance arrangement.

Sources for Narrative

This new narrative basically relied on the speech Jawaharlal Nehru delivered in Nagore in Rajasthan while inaugurating Panchayati Raj in India on 2nd October, 1959[9], speech delivered by S.K. Dey in Bangalore while participating in All India Panchayat Parishad Annual Convention after the demise of Nehru and the speech delivered by Jayaprakash Narayan on 18th July, 1964 in the same conference.[10] This will enable the researcher to look at the new system of governance envisioned by Pandit Jawaharlal Nehru at the grassroots in a proper perspective as perspective plays a major role in shaping the institutional design for effective and efficient delivery of services and empowerment of the poor and the marginalized. The Constituent Assembly debates on Panchayati Raj[11] will bring to light the intellectual discourse held in the country while carving out the governance system for the community at the dawn of Independence based on the social reality. This will be much helpful for a realistic analysis of the conditions with which decision for the creation of Panchayati Raj in India was taken. The speech delivered by Nehru in Nagore, Chennai and a few other places on Panchayati Raj gives the framework for the New

Panchayati Raj System after establishment of the new governance arrangement in India.[12] The speech of the S.K. Dey would reflect the operationalization of the framework given by Nehru as S.K. Dey served as Minister in the Nehru's cabinet. Jayaprakash Narayan's speech will reflect the problems he faced as leader of the Gandhian Movement worked for the establishment of Panchayati Raj System in India by synthesizing the framework of Nehru with the framework of Gandhi. The whole discourse will help us to understand the power of the social and bureaucratic forces in shaping democracy, and other governance arrangement at the grassroots.

Foundational Narrative

Jawaharlal Nehru was facing a criticism that he was not taking forward the Panchayati Raj System envisioned by Mahatma Gandhi when he was in power at the dawn of Independence. Because in the whole process of Constitutional debates, Panchayati Raj had not been pushed to the centre stage and it was taken up for consideration only at the end as the omission of it was pointed out by M.K. Gandhi. It is a known fact that within the short span of time, evolving a governance framework suitable to diverse socio-economic cultural settings of different region is not an ordinary task. In the given context, what could be achieved had been done in the Constitution. The time and context constraints prevented the Constitution Makers to evolve a comprehensive framework for local governance to govern rural India at that point of time. The whole responsibility of creating a vibrant rural local body system was on the shoulders of Jawaharlal Nehru. Reality of the villages in India projected by Dr. B.R. Ambedkar cannot be brushed aside. Dr. B.R. Ambedkar's villages are the reality, but M.K. Gandhi's villages are only vision and dreams. Nehru has to act realistically to take the villages from the reality to the new vision. This transformative process could not be achieved through a simple administrative mechanism and processes. It required a hard decision with tough follow up. Gandhian framework of politics and economics has been conceptualized only as rhetoric, but not in action. Till India got Independence the whole freedom movement followed the path of Gandhi. The moment India got Independence it moved away from the track of Gandhi. This had been witnessed at the dawn of Independence after the establishment of the governance arrangement in India. Nehru was keen in bringing this subject again not as rhetoric, but as a fact. The moment he initiated steps to establish Panchayati Raj the slur on his name has been removed. He created a Ministry for Community Development, Panchayati Raj and Cooperation and guided the Ministry to take forward the new system of governance at the community level throughout India. How he nurtured Panchayati Raj was explained by S.K. Dey after the demise of Nehru in Bangalore while he was delivering a lecture in the convention of the All India Panchayat Parishad. He himself stated that he carried out instructions of Jawaharlal Nehru in building grassroots democracy in India. It was Nehru's vision that was translated into action by the Ministry. Nehru outlined the functions and responsibilities of the new governance structure in his address when he inaugurated the Panchayati Raj in Nagore, Rajasthan. It is considered as basic text of Nehru's Panchayati Raj System of India. From an analysis of the framework one can gauge what kind of system he wanted to create at the bottom.

While considering the tasks for New Panchayati Raj he made an unequivocal plea that nation building exercise has to be done from the bottom and for which politically people have to be made conscious and they have to be mobilized. The above task has to be performed by the Panchayats as per his vision. He unequivocally called the people to engage themselves to reconstruct India. People of India should have all necessities of life. All these things could be achieved only through hard work and not through charity. By making this statement Nehru underlined the importance of dignity, empowerment and entitlement of the people in the rural areas. He said that "India will make real progress only when the people living in villages become politically conscious." He wanted to raise the consciousness of the people as he defined development as consciousness. The reason for making this statement is that people should be politically conscientized and by which an informed citizenry could be created. The basic assumption is that an informed citizenry will create enlightened activities at the community level. People at the grassroots have to take more responsibilities and by which they should be in a position to make the Government machinery accountable to them. At Panchayat level responsibilities of administration should be handed over to the people. By continuous engagement of the people in development and governance people will always be at the centre and as a result there will not be any gap between the Government machinery and the people. People nearer to the government will empower people and reduce corruption and Government will be made accountable to the people. Hence, he emphasises continuous engagement of the people in development and governance. The whole argument projected above can be epitomized as trust in people. His faith in Indian masses is unshakable. It is to be recognized that there is a quite opposite view from Nehruvian days to present. It was elaborated by Jayaprakash Narayan in his Bangalore address after the demise of Nehru. Here one has to look at the broader and narrower view of decentralization. Broader view of decentralization refers to the establishment of institutional mechanism for governance and work for economic development through a process of involvement of the citizens. It requires citizens and more specifically the informed citizens. Law of subsidiarity will be the base for such a kind of activities. Narrower perspective of local governance or decentralization or Panchayati Raj refers to entrustment of some responsibilities of the Government departments to the local bodies to deliver certain services to the people. There was a school of thought considered that local bodies are considered as mere implementing agencies of the Central and State Governments. Because there was no Government down below the State. There was no boundary fixed for local government. Law-making power was not given to local bodies. Hence, at the maximum the local bodies can play a role of an implementing agency. Broader view of decentralization essentially encompasses deepening of democracy, empowering people and achieving economic development. The above could be done only when citizens are mobilized, consceintised and involved in all kinds of development activities. Citizenship building is crucial to strengthening of local government and local democracy. Basically, it is a democracy promotional activity.[13]

Nehru had taken a broader perspective of building up of local democratic institutions and processes, enabling the community to achieve economic development, and achieving higher consciousness. These are the two essential functions of the Panchayati Raj Institutions in India. Nehru's vision of Panchayati Raj is not only a broader perspective of decentralization and it moves beyond it as people's movement. Its boundaries are human capabilities. While putting this argument he knew the conditions and consciousness level of the people at the ground. He knew that country came out from a worst crisis of religious conflicts because of the creation of Pakistan and the emerging ethic, caste and social conflicts in Indian society. Yet, he found representative democracy was the only option for redeeming the situation. While carving out institution for government he wanted to give a link between the state and the people through local governance process. In his opinion people have to build a vision for India. They have to work for the nation through local action. This could be possible only by enhancing the level of consciousness of the people. Thus, people have to play both the citizenship role, namely community citizenship and Constitutional citizenship. According to him the idea of Indian nation should become the integral part of the activities of the people. In this context, he lamented that people have to be conscientized emotionally for the cause of the country. He recalled the exercises the leaders have done during the freedom struggle. People have perished themselves their differences for the cause of the nation. They entertained a new hope in the new nation. It has to continue to achieve development for all. It needs larger people's engagement. In this way peoples larger attachment has to be activated. While analyzing the first part of his speech, one can easily identify the logic behind it. He wanted to link it with oceanic circle theory of M.K. Gandhi. People have to take part in the affairs of the country only through a process of engagement at the grassroots. It has to start from Panchayat. Basically, Nehru wanted the Gandhian framework of Gram Swaraj to be fixed into the established representative democratic government at the Centre and the States. It is to be noted here that there was an argument in the Constituent Assembly that it will take time to evolve such a framework for Panchayati Raj to suit the requirements of the community. Article 40 came out based on the above argument. But Nehru made it clear that "the responsibilities of administration should not be in the hands of big officials only but they should be divided equally aiming our 400 million people." It will bring strength. It is a learning process. He considered people are the strength, however, they are poor or illiterate. His trust and faith in people is unshakable. Hence, he wanted a dynamic institutional framework at the ground for the engagement of the people. He designed institutions synergistically at the grassroots. They are Panchayati Raj, cooperatives and primary schools. They are the trinities of local democratic governance and development paradigm. They have to work together to reconstruct the communities, rebuild the economy and to conscientise the people on development and democracy. Panchayati Raj is to establish governance, and enable people to participate in governance. Cooperative is a growth engine and primary schools are to conscientise and educate the people.

He made it clear that the design of the cooperative institution should not be a prototype for the whole of the country. It should not be in a conventional type of institutions. It should move beyond credit to farmers. Cooperative should be the centre of economic activities. The cooperative institutions are of different kinds. In his perspective they should be allowed to function independently in consultation with stakeholders. While designing the cooperatives, Nehru in unequivocal terms explained that the functions of a cooperative society should depend upon the needs and conditions of the area in which it is formed. In his perspective cooperative institutions should have enough scope for activities based on the vision and needs of the communities in which they function. How to run the cooperative union is the key question as it has lot of hopes and visions? To realize the same he suggested training for the leaders, representatives and officials on managing the cooperative institutions in an innovative way based on the needs of the area and the stakeholders. Nehru's vision of cooperative union is broader and it has got a perspective.

He tried his level best to operationalize the Gandhian framework of Gram Swaraj. He lamented that in India our farmers are having small land holdings and they are deprived of the opportunity of using modern technologies for agriculture. Everyone knows in the absence of adoption of modern technologies and scientific farm practices, agriculture output cannot be increased and profit out of agriculture will not be increased. How to help farmers to adopt modern technologies is the key issue? He suggested that the cooperative should take such a kind of responsibility. Making the farmers to use technologies for increasing production lies in the hands of the cooperatives. The cooperatives should have the abilities, capacities and capabilities to extend all kinds of handhold support to the small farmers for their farm production and marketing activities. It is not only an engine to provide credit, but also to extend ideas, vision and innovation. It has to protect the farmers from exploitation. Hence, he argued that it should enjoy independence, and autonomy to meet the requirements of the local small farmers. From the above argument one can easily understand that what kind of Panchayati Raj System he wanted? Cooperatives and Panchayats cannot be seen in isolation. They are the two powerful institutional mechanism work for political and economic democracy.

The third pillar he carved out in the framework is school for education. It is not education for children alone. People in the villages are in need of education as people have to go with time. Transformation has to be created and managed and for which education is necessary. Education is key for people to lead a decent, dignified, scientific and happy human life. While doing so, he reiterated the fact that it should be for both men and women. In this context, he emphatically argued that women not only to contribute for family welfare, but also to the nation. Education is necessary for them to move out from homes and to integrate them with the society. He argued that the establishment of school is not only to increase the literacy rate. He reiterated the fact that every rural populace needs education. To make use of the new opportunities for development, villagers need education. To transform the conditions of the rural life villagers need education. His concept of school is not linking to literacy alone. It is an institutional mechanism to transform the community to lead a scientific human life.

He emphatically stated that Panchayats, Cooperatives and Schools are the three pillars of village life. How to bring synergy among these institutions is yet another question-answered by Jawaharlal Nehru. In his lengthy inaugural address he mentioned at least how our elected representatives and officials have to work in this transformational process. He brought in the concept of democracy and its core value 'equality' in the transformational process. He indicated that the society is liberated from the colonial yoke jointly by the rich and the poor. It raised the image of the Indian society. In the same way, Indian society has to work for achieving development for the people. It is a process of bringing the social energy for reconstructing the society and economy. It needs strategies. The strategy is to work with others and working together. He argued that the people of India have demonstrated to the world that by uniting together by subsuming all the differences India was liberated. In the same way people of India have to demonstrate to the world that they would work for liberating people from poverty and achieving prosperity. A new transformational model has to be evolving through this local institution by involving the people. This is not an isolated event. It needs collective efforts, organizational and institutional efforts. It needs a new mindset. Unless one has that mindset, it is very difficult to maintain equality. Officials and the elected representatives have to give up the tendency of dominating each other. The spirit of equality is the need to get the cooperation of every segment of the society. He further mentioned that in India everyone is equal politically as everyone has got one vote. Through the democratic practice of maintaining equality in the governance process social equality has to be achieved. Economic equality has to be achieved by providing opportunities for economic development of the households. He has underlined the equality of economic opportunities to the poor by the Panchayat and Cooperative Organizations. Finally, he made a fervent plea that everyone should be involved in raising consciousness among the people to lay a movement for democracy and development. In this context, he touched upon the core values of democracy. Equality, respecting the dissent voice, fairness, justice, and equity have to be intact in the activities of the Panchayats. Here, one has to understand why Nehru always underlines the importance of consciousness. He, in fact, wanted to engage the people for the purpose of elevating them from the practices which were antithetical to democracy and leading scientific human life. This process is not so easy. It requires leadership. Hence, he reiterated the need of training for the people who are taking responsibilities in Panchayats and Cooperatives. The training which he mentioned is transformational in nature and character.

Democratization and development engagement are the twin objectives incorporated into the framework of Panchayati Raj envisaged by Nehru. His conviction stems from the argument that unless people are involved in the process of governance and development however weak they are, one cannot build full citizenship among the people. It needs leadership for Panchayati Raj and Cooperative Institutions. The tasks assigned to the grassroots institutions are huge. There is no demarcation as stipulated in 11th Schedule. To carry out the above tasks the leaders of local bodies and cooperative unions require skill, capacity and capability. It is a major question whether steps have been taken at different levels to shape transformational leadership at the grassroots level. In a caste ridden hierarchical society with feudal and patriarchical mindset, decentralization and democratization have to cross huge barriers in the process. Because decentralization and democratization will deal with power equation and it requires a new mindset and behaviour among the people who keep power with them for a long. To create such a condition, a movement has to be built up from below. This new movement could be built up by the efforts of the transformational leaders. The country witnessed sea of transformational leaders trained through a life process in M.K. Gandhi's Ashram. Such Ashrams could have been converted into training centres for the preparation of transformational leaders. Unfortunately, it did not take place.

Evolving a suitable framework of local governance based on the vision of M.K. Gandhi and fitting into the larger framework of governance modelled on the West is not a simple task. It requires huge mobilization of masses more than the mobilization of masses for freedom struggle. Since, faith in state system gained currency at the dawn of Independence, decentralization could not attract and draw the attention of the society. But after thirty years of experience of the big state approach the whole world started moving towards decentralization as the big government approach failed.[14] Even in subsequent wave of decentralization one would find barriers and obstacles. Hence, it becomes only rhetoric not a fact. Decentralization is inevitable. It cannot be resisted. The major problem in decentralization is that governments are committed yet it is only in philosophy and not in fact. It is because most of the Governments are not interested in taking hard decisions in reshaping taxation, expenditure, borrowing and budgetary powers.[15] It is also established that rural economic activities have contributed for economic development of the country.[16] While looking at the vision, framework of decentralization conceptualized by our Founding Fathers and the experiences what we gained sofar in our country, one has to recognize the struggle of the leaders. Because from M.K. Gandhi to Jayaprakash Narayan the global conditions and local conditions were totally against the decentralization process. But when Rajiv Gandhi reconceptualized the decentralization through constitutionalization, the global conditions are favourable to decentralization.[17] More than sixty countries took earnest efforts to introduce decentralization. The institutions which shape economic activities in the world come out openly that decentralization is the only way to create a new world social order. Countries cannot escape from decentralization. It becomes inevitable now. These are all positive factors for decentralization now. But these factors were not present at the dawn of Independence. We had leaders with vision, ideas, and commitment at the dawn of Independence. But conditions were not conducive for transformation. Now, conditions are favourable for transformation, but we find dearth of leadership in the political sphere to move further.[18]

Conclusion

Jawaharlal Nehru took a broader perspective of democratic decentralization. His vision of Panchayati Raj is not only for governance and administration of service delivery, but also for building a vibrant rural economy emerging from agriculture and to integrate it with industrial economy. It is meant for social transformation and economic development. The tasks assigned to Panchayati Raj System are huge and the institutions are meant for engaging the public. It is aimed at empowering the people by raising the voice of the poor, and the marginalized. The tasks assigned to the Panchayats are heavy and they are to be internalized and conscientized by the leaders of Panchayati Raj. What he expected from the leaders of Panchayati Raj is not mere management of services, but more of innovation for economic development. The leadership what he conceptualized was transformational in nature. Nehru wanted to integrate the key elements of the framework of Gram Swaraj of M.K. Gandhi with representative democratic system established for governance in India through the Constitution. It is unfortunate that the governance system established at the Centre and State had not developed proper perspective and system to integrate Nehru's vision on Panchayati Raj. It is yet another failure that the Gandhian institutions and leaders had not mobilized people to build a strong people's movement for Gram Swaraj. The forces which were and are against decentralization had always been powerful and systematic. But the forces which were and are for decentralization had always been fragile and weak and sporadic. Althrough it is a struggle between state and the people, poor and rich and dominant and oppressed. The poor and the oppressed could win through a process of struggle by using decentralization and democratization. To achieve the above what we need is democracy promotion, transformational leadership creation and building up of a strong intellectual movement along with peoples' movement.

NOTES

1. Myron Weiner, 1989, *Indian Paradox,* New Delhi: Sage Publications, pp. 21-37.
2. Christophe Jaffrelot, 2012, "The Paradoxical Democratization of Indian Democracy" in Christophe Jaffrelot (ed.) *India Since 1950: Society, Politics, Economy and Culture,* New Delhi: Foundation Books, pp. 55-83.
3. S.M. Vijayanand, Secretary, Government of India, delivered A.K. Venkatasubramanian Endowment Lecure on 5th November, 2015 in Gandhigram Rural Institute on Social Democracy. In his lecture he emphasized that the benefit of political democracy could be enjoyed by the poor only when social democracy is created at the grassroots. Social democracy could be achieved at present through the Panchayati Raj System and the rising power of women through SHG.
4. Philip Keefer, "Poor Performance of Poor Democracies" in Charles Boix and Susan C. Stokes (eds.) *The Oxford Handbook of Comparative Politics,* New Delhi: Oxford University Press, 2009, pp. 886-909.
5. Ravinder Kumar, 1998, Democracy: From Consolidation to Fluidity in Hiranmay Karlekar (ed.), *Independent India: The First Fifty Years,* New Delhi: Oxford University Press, pp. 3-15.
6. Peter Burnell, 2008, "Promoting Democracy" in Daniele Caramani (ed.) *Comparative Politics,* New Delhi: Oxford University Press.
7. K.C. Sivaramakrishnan, 2000, Power to the People? *The Politics and Progress of Decentralization,* New Delhi: Konarka Publishers.
8. Mani Shankar Aiyar, 2013, *Towards Holistic Panchayati Raj: Twentieth Anniversary Report of the Expert Committee on Leveraging Panchayats for Efficient Delivery of Public Goods and Services,* Vols. I & II, New Delhi: Government of India.

9. Inaugural Address of Jawaharlal Nehru in Nagore, Rajasthan on 2nd October, 1959 while inaugurating the Panchayati Raj, *All India Congress Committee Economic Review 1960* (The speech was in Hindi. It was translated into English).
10. Special address by A.K. Dey, then Minister for Community Development and Panchayati Raj in the Fourth National All India Panchayat Parishad Conference, Bangalore on 18th July, 1964; Presidential Address of Jayaprakash Narayan, in the Fourth National All India Panchayat Parishad Conference, Bangalore on 18th July, 1964; All India Panchayat Parishad, *Panchayati Raj: Perspective and Programme,* New Delhi: All India Panchayat Parishad, 1965.
11. Association of Voluntary Agencies for Rural Development, 1962, *Panchayati Raj as the Basis of Indian Polity,* New Delhi: Association of Voluntary Agencies for Rural Development.
12. Government of India, 1965, *Jawaharlal Nehru on Community Development, Panchayati Raj and Cooperation,* New Delhi: Ministry of Community Development and Cooperation.
13. Many of the Western countries kept democracy promotional activity as one of the aspects of their foreign policy and allocated huge resources for democracy promotion activities through local bodies in the developing countries. For more details see Peter Burnell "Promoting Democracy" in Daniele Caramani (ed.), 2008, *Comparative Politics,* New York: Oxford University Press, pp. 625-650.
14. Hans Binswanger Mkhize, De Regt, Jacomina P. and Stephen Spector, *Local and Community Driven Development: Moving to Scale in Theory and Practice,* Washington DC: World Bank, 2010; Mansuri G.V. Rao, *Localizing Development: Does Participation Work?* Washington DC: World Bank, 2012; Sheri Torjman and Anne Makhoul, *Community Led Development,* Ottawa: Caledon Institute of Social Policy, 2012; The Hunger Project, 2014 *State of Participatory Democracy Report,* New York: The Hunger Project, 2014.
15. Shahid, Yusuf, 2000, Weiping Wn, Simon Evenelt (eds.) *Local Dynamics in an Era of Globalization,* New York: Oxford University Press, pp. 94-113.
16. David de Ferranti, Guillermo E., Perry, William Foster, Daniel Ledesman, Alberto Valdes, (eds.) 2005, *Beyond the City: The Rural Contribution to Development,* Washington DC: The World Bank, pp. 61-102.
17. James Manor, 1999, *Political Economy of Democratic Decentralization,* Washington DC: The World Bank.
18. Leadership is crucial for any transformation. Leadership enhancement is a difficult task to be performed. Leadership school of a different order is the need of the day. For more details on leadership see, Peter, G. Northouse, 2007, *Leadership: Theory and Practice,* New Delhi: Sage Publications.

Bibliography

Association of Voluntary Agencies for Rural Development (1962), *Panchayati Raj as the Basis of Indian Polity*, New Delhi: Association of Voluntary Agencies for Rural Development.

Baechler, Jean (1998), *Democracy: An Analytical Survey*, New Delhi: National Book Trust, India.

Bardhan, Pranab and Mookherjee, Dilip, (eds.) (2007) *Decentralization and Local Governance in Developing Countries: A Comparative Perspective*, New Delhi: Oxford University Press.

Basu, Kaushik (2007), *The Retreat of Democracy*, Ranikhet: Permanent Black.

Burnell, Peter (2008), "Promoting Democracy" in Daniele Caramani (ed.) *Comparative Politics*, New Delhi: Oxford University Press.

Carl Wright, "Decentralization and Development: Experience from the Commonwealth Countries" in the Thinkers Conference organized by Kerala Institute of Local Administration in Trissur, Kerala on 20th and 21st January, 2016.

Crick, Bernard (2002), *Democracy: A Very Short Introduction*, New Delhi: Oxford University Press.

Dahl, Robert A., (1972), *Authority in a Good Society: After the Revolution?* New Delhi: Allied Publishers Private Limited.

David de Ferranti, Guillermo E., Perry, William Foster, Daniel Ledesman, Alberto Valdes (eds.) (2005), *Beyond the City: The Rural Contribution to Development*, Washington DC: The World Bank, pp. 61-102.

Deininger, K., Nagarajan, H., and Paul, S., (2012) "Can Political Reservations Empower Women and Affect Economic Outcomes? Evidence from Rural India" *NCAER working papers on Decentralization and Rural Governance in India* No. 4; S. Kaushik

(1998), *Participation of Women in Panchayati Raj in India: A Stock Taking*, New Delhi: National Commission for Women.

Denhardt, Janet V., and Denhardt, Robert (2011), "Leadership" in Bevir, Mark (ed.) *The Sage Handbook of Governance*, New Delhi: Sage Publications.

Fumihiko Saito (2011), "Decentralization" in Mark Bevir (ed.) *The Sage Handbook of Governance*, Washington DC: Sage Publications, pp. 484-500.

Gandhi, M.K. (1960), *Hind Swaraj*, Ahamedabad: Navjeevan Publications.

Geddes, Barabara (2009), "What Causes Democratization?" in Charles Boix and Susan C. Stokes (eds.), *The Oxford Handbook of Comparative Politics*, New Delhi: Oxford University Press.

Ginsborg, Paul (2009), *Democracy: Crisis and Renewal*, London: Profile Books Ltd.

Government of India (1965), *Jawaharlal Nehru on Community Development, Panchayati Raj and Cooperation*, New Delhi: Ministry of Community Development and Cooperation.

Government of India (1994), *The 73rd Amendment to the Constitution of India*, New Delhi: Ministry of Rural Development.

Government of India (2001), *Report of the Task Force on Panchayati Raj Institutions*, New Delhi: Government of India.

Government of India (2002), *Report of National Commission to Review the Working of the Constitution*, Vols. I and II, New Delhi: Ministry of Law, Justice and Company Affairs.

Government of India (2006), *The State of the Panchayats: A Mid-Term Review and Appraisal 2006*, New Delhi: Ministry of Panchayati Raj, 2006; Government of India, *Report of the Working Group on Democratic Decentralization and Panchayati Raj Institutions*, New Delhi: Planning Commission, Government of India.

Government of India (2007), "*Local Governance: An Inspiring Journey to the Future*" Vol. II, *Second Administrative Reforms Commissions Report*", New Delhi: Government of India.

Government of India (2008), *Study on Elected Women Representatives in Panchayati Raj Institutions*, New Delhi: Ministry of Panchayati Raj.

Government of India (2010), *Compilation of Important Correspondence and Minutes of Major Meetings*, New Delhi: Ministry of Panchayati Raj.

Government of India (2015), *Fourteenth Finance Commission*, New Delhi: Ministry of Finance.

Government of India (2015), *Guidelines for the Implementation of Recommendation of Fourteenth Finance Commission with Regard to Local Bodies* No. 13 (32) FFC/FCD/2015-16, New Delhi: Ministry of Finance.

Government of India (2015), *Unnata Bharat Abhiyan* [F. No. 19-8/2014-TS-1 (sec)] New Delhi: Ministry of Human Resource Development.

Government of India, *Report of the Second Commission on Centre-State Relations*, Vols. I & II, New Delhi: Government of India.

Gupta, D.G. (2004), *Decentralization: Need for Reform*, New Delhi: Concept Publishing Company.

Hans, Binswanger Mkhize, De, Regt, Jacomina, P. and Stephen, Spector (2010), *Local and Community Driven Development: Moving to Scale in Theory and Practice*, Washington DC: World Bank; Mansuri Rao, G.V. (2012), *Localizing Development: Does Participation Work?*, Washington DC: World Bank; Sheri Torjman and Anne Makhoul (2012), *Community Led Development*, Ottawa: Caledon Institute of Social Policy; The Hunger Project (2014), 2014 *State of Participatory Democracy Report*, New York: The Hunger Project.

In Rajiv Gandhi Chair we took initiative to prepare manual for administration. Palanithurai, G. (2011), *Tamil Nadu Rural Local Bodies: Responsibilities and Process (Tamil) Manual for Local Body Leaders*, Chennai: Bharathi Puthakalayam; Palanithurai, G. and *et al.* (2006), *Handbook of Tamil Nadu Panchayat Administration*, New Delhi: Concept Publishing Company.

Inaugural Address of Jawaharlal Nehru in Nagore, Rajasthan on 2nd October, 1959 while inaugurating the Panchayati Raj, *All India Congress Committee Economic Review*, 1960 (The speech was in Hindi. It was translated into English).

Jaffrelot, Christophe (2012), "The Paradoxical Democratization of Indian Democracy" in Jaffrelot, Christophe (ed.) *India Since 1950: Society, Politics, Economy and Culture*, New Delhi: Foundation Books, pp. 55-83.

Jayal, Niraja Gopal (2006), "Introduction" in Jayal, Niraja Gopal, Prakash, Amit and Sharma, Pradeep K. (eds.), *Local Governance in India: Decentralization and Beyond*, New Delhi: Oxford University Press.

Keefer, Philip (2009), "Poor Performance of Poor Democracies" in Charles Boix and Susan C. Stokes (eds.) *The Oxford Handbook of Comparative Politics*, New Delhi: Oxford University Press, pp. 886-909.

Kothari, Rajani (2005), *Rethinking Democracy*, Hyderabad: Orient Longman.

Kumar, Ravinder (1998), "Democracy: From Consolidation to Fluidity" in Karlekar, Hiranmay (ed.), *Independent India: The Finest Fifty Years*, New Delhi: Oxford University Press.

Leadership is crucial for any transformation. Leadership enhancement is a difficult task to be performed. Leadership school of a different order is the need of the day. For more details on leadership see, Peter G. Northouse (2007), *Leadership: Theory and Practice*, New Delhi: Sage Publications.

Lijphart, Arend (1989), *Democracy in Plural Societies: A Comparative Exploration*, Bombay: Popular Prakashan.

Mair, Peter (2008), "Democracies" in Daniele Caramani (ed.), *Comparative Politics*, New Delhi: Oxford University Press.

Mani Shankar Aiyar (2013), *Towards Holistic Panchayati Raj: Twentieth Anniversary Report of the Expert Committee on Leveraging Panchayats for Efficient Delivery of Public Goods and Services*, Vols. I & II, New Delhi: Government of India.

Mani Shankar Aiyar, 2016, "In the Backdrop of Global Experience India's experience in Decentralization", Special lecture in the Thinkers Conference organized by Kerala Institute of Local Administration in Trissur, Kerala on 20th and 21st January.

Manor, James (1999), *Political Economy of Democratic Decentralization*, Washington DC: The World Bank.

Manor, James (2010), "Local Governance" in Niraja Gopal Jayal and Pratap Bhanu Mehta (eds.) *The Oxford Companion to Politics in India*, New Delhi: Oxford University Press, pp. 61-79.

Manor, James (2012), "Perspectives on Decentralization" in *The Imperative of Good Local Governance: Challenges of the Next Decade of Decentralization* (eds.) Joakim Ojendal and Ankis Delinas, United States: United Nations University Press.

Many of the western countries kept democracy promotional activity as one of the aspects of their foreign policy and allocated huge resources for democracy promotion activities through local bodies in the developing countries. For more details see Peter Burnell "Promoting Democracy" in Daniele Caramani (ed.) (2008) *Comparative Politics*, New York: Oxford University Press, pp. 625-650.

Marks, Gray and DiaMond Larry (eds.), (1992), *Reexamining Democracy*, New Delhi: Sage Publications.

Mathew, G. and Buch, N. (2011) (eds.), *Status of Panchayati Raj in the States and Union Territories in India*, New Delhi: Concept Publishing Company (P) Ltd.

McLaverty, Peter (2011), "Participation" in Bevir, Mark (ed.) *The Sage Handbook of Governance*, New Delhi: Sage Publications.

Ministry of Panchayati Raj (2008), *Study on Elected Women Representatives in Panchayati Raj Institutions*, New Delhi: Government of India.

Nagarajan, Hari K., Hans, P. Binswanger Mkhize and Meenakshisundaram, S.S. (2015), *Decentralization and Empowerment for Rural Development*, New Delhi: Foundation Books.

Narayan, Jayaprakash (1964), "Presidential Speech" in All India Panchayat Parishad, *Panchayati Raj: Perspective and Programme*, New Delhi: All India Panchayat Parishad.

Order F. No. 19-8/2014–TS.1 (Sectt.), Government of India, Ministry of Human Resource Development, Department of Higher Education, Dated: 24th August, 2015 (*Unnat Bharat Abhiyan*).

Order No. 13 (32) FFC/FCD/2015-16, Government of India, Ministry of Finance, Department of Expenditure (Finance Commission Division) dated: 8th October, 2015. Guidelines for the implementations of recommendations of Fourteenth for Finance Commission (FC XIV) with regard to local bodies grant.

Palanithurai, G. (2012), *Elected Women Representatives and Empowerment*, New Delhi: Concept Publishing Company (P) Ltd.

Palanithurai, G. (2013), *Dalits and Dalit Representatives in Rural Local Governance: Voices from the Field*, New Delhi: Concept Publishing Company (P) Ltd.

Palanithurai G. (ed.) (2015), *Deliberative Democracy*, New Delhi: MJP Publishers.

Palanithurai, G. Thirunavukkarasu, M.A. and Uma, G. (2008), *Change Makers at Grassroots*, New Delhi: Concept Publishing Company (P) Ltd.

Palanithurai, G. (2009), *Panchayat in Disaster Preparedness and Management*, New Delhi: Concept Publishing Company (P) Ltd.

Palanithurai, G. (2014), *Governance Issues in India: From Grassroots Perspective*, New Delhi: Concept Publishing Company (P) Ltd.

Palanithurai, G. (ed.) (2014), *Federating Elected Women Representatives of Local Bodies in India*, New Delhi: Concept Publishing Company (P) Ltd.

Parekh, Bhikhu (2011), "The Crisis in Indian Democracy", Jawaharlal Nehru Memorial Lecture delivered in Trinity College on 21st November.

Paul Faguet, Jean and Posche, Caroline (2015) (eds.), *Is Decentralization Good for Development? Perspectives from Academics and Policy Makers*, London: Oxford University Press.

Paul Faguet, Jean, 2016, "Decentralization Promises and Performances" in the Thinkers Conference organized by Kerala Institute of Local Administration in Trissur, Kerala on 20th and 21st January.

Presidential Address of Jayaprakash Narayan in the Fourth National All India Panchayat Parishad Conference, Bangalore on 18th July, 1964. All India Panchayati Parishad, *Panchayati Raj: Perspective and Programme,* New Delhi: All India Panchayat Parishad, 1965.

PRIA (2001), *The State of Panchayats,* New Delhi: PRIA.

Rajiv Gandhi Chair (2007), *Ten Years of Decentralization Activities,* Gandhigram: Rajiv Gandhi Chair for Panchayati Raj Studies.

Singh, Satyajit (2007), "Introduction" in Singh, Satyajit and Sharma Pradeep, K. (eds.) *Decentralization: Institutions and Politics in Rural India,* New Delhi: Oxford University Press.

Sivaramakrishnan, K.C. (2000), Power to the People? *The Politics and Progress of Decentralization,* New Delhi: Konark Publishers.

Special address by A.K. Dey, then Minister for Community Development and Panchayati Raj in the Fourth National All India Panchayat Parishad Conference, Bangalore on 18th July, 1964; Presidential Address of Jayaprakash Narayan, in the Fourth National All India Panchayat Parishad Conference, Bangalore on 18th July, 1964; All India Panchayat Parishad, *Panchayati Raj: Perspective and Programme,* New Delhi: All India Panchayat Parishad, 1965.

Tata Institute of Social Sciences (2015), *Devolution Report 2014-15: How Effective in Devolution Across Indian States Insights from the Field,* New Delhi: Ministry of Panchayati Raj, Government of India.

Tata Institute of Social Sciences (2015), *How Effective in Devolution across Indian States: Insights from the Field Devolution Report 2014-15,* New Delhi: Ministry of Panchayati Raj, Government of India.

Thomassen, Jacques (2009), "Democratic Values" Russel J. Dalton and Klingemann, Hans-Dieter (eds.), *The Oxford Hand Book of Political Behaviour,* New York: Oxford University Press.

Vijayanand, S.M., 2016, "Decentralization Experience in Kerala" special lecture in the Thinkers Conference organized by Kerala Institute of Local Administration in Trissur, Kerala on 20th and 21st January.

Vijayanand, S.M., 2015, Secretary, Government of India delivered A.K. Venkatasubramanian Endowment Lecture on 5th November, in Gandhigram Rural Institute on Social Democracy. In his lecture he emphasized that the benefit of political democracy could be enjoyed by the poor only when social democracy is created at the grassroots.

Social democracy could be achieved at present through the Panchayati Raj system and the rising power of women through SHG.

Vora, Rajendra and Palshikar, Suhas (eds.), (2004), *Indian Democracy Meanings and Practices,* New Delhi: Sage Publications.

Weiner, Myron (1989), *The Indian Paradox: Essays in Indian Politics,* New Delhi: Sage Publications.

World Bank (2008), *Decentralization in Client Countries: An Evaluation of World Bank Support 1990 to 2007,* Washington DC: World Bank.

Yusuf Shahid, Wn Weiping, Evenelt Simon (eds.), (2000), *Local Dynamics in an Era of Globalization,* New York: Oxford University Press, pp. 94-113.

Index